OPENING NEW DOORS:
Alternative Careers for Librarians

Edited by Ellis Mount

Special Libraries Association
1993

Library of Congress Cataloging-in-Publication Data

Opening New Doors: Alternative Careers for Librarians/edited
by Ellis Mount.
          p. cm.
      Includes bibliographical references and index.
      ISBN 0-87111-408-9
      1. Library science—Vocational guidance—United
States.
2.   Information science—Vocational guidance—United
States.
I.   Mount, Ellis.
Z682.2.U5065   1992
020'.23'73—dc20

Cover design by
Anita Winfield

1993 by Special Libraries Association
1700 Eighteenth Street, N.W.
Washington, DC 20009-2508

Manufactured in the United States of America.
ISBN 0-87111-408-9

PREFACE

This book aims at broadening the horizons of those people who have been trained to work in traditional libraries but who want to consider other ways to use their library training and experience. The chapters are written by experienced people in successful careers that use their library backgrounds but also involve them in new activities, often far removed from what they may have envisioned when they became librarians.

I am grateful for the cooperation of the twenty eight authors who agreed to write chapters for this book. Without their help, there would have been no book. I hope that these accounts of their experiences will serve to encourage others to consider new careers and open new doors for themselves.

Ellis Mount

TABLE OF CONTENTS

viii

AN OVERVIEW

by ELLIS MOUNT

It is not unusual for people to work in fields for which they were not specifically trained and educated. For example, an airline pilot might become head of long-range planning for a major airline; a schoolteacher might leave the classroom and become the director of the training department for a corporation that teaches certain skills to new employees. The purpose of this book, to describe unusual jobs held by individuals who were trained for traditional positions normally filled by librarians, is not unique. However, the twenty eight chapters provided here may surprise those readers who were not aware of the many opportunities available to people with library backgrounds.

People leave the familiar library environment to seek employment elsewhere for two major reasons. First, some may have difficulty finding a job opening in a library. As this book was being prepared, budgets in all types of libraries were cut back, often resulting in staff reductions or hiring freezes. While we hope that this situation will change, such change is not apt to happen quickly. Many would-be librarians are forced to look elsewhere for employment.

The second reason is that some people who could work in traditional libraries have preferred different careers, perhaps using their library skills and experience in ways they could never have envisioned when they finished their education. In most instances they feel very satisfied in their new careers and do not want to go back to traditional libraries.

The remainder of this book is divided into two parts. Part II consists of twelve chapters written by entrepreneurs, who have created their own positions. Some work alone, such as the information brokers who serve a variety of clients. Others have created their own companies and subsequently hired people to work for them.

Part III comprises sixteen chapters written by people who have left traditional library positions and are working in organizations owned by other people. These organizations range from publishing firms to developers of internationally known databases. Some of the authors represented in this section work for associations created to help libraries.

Each chapter includes four major points: a description of how the author became involved in his or her new career; the nature of the work; the qualifications required for success; and the advantages and disadvantages of this type of work.

In almost every case the authors were originally trained in conventional library schools. The one or two exceptions are people who were not formally trained in librarianship but who readily recognize that library skills would have been useful in their careers. These individuals did come from a library background, even if they were not specifically trained for such work.

Each chapter represents a serious employment opportunity. I have a librarian friend who is a drummer in a rock band in her spare time, and earns money at it. But it is essentially a hobby for her, not a means of earning a living. Such activities are not included here. All of the authors have considerable experience in their new fields and thus can write authoritatively about their work.

With the growing inclusion in traditional library schools of education and training in information science, more and more of their graduates now are thinking about careers outside the traditional ones. As this trend continues, it will no longer be easy to define the careers of library and information program graduates. Growth in computer-based communication, and management jobs is already having an effect on the work available to "traditional librarians." In time it may become taken for granted that library and information science schools prepare their graduates for a wider range of positions. A compilation such as this one may become difficult to prepare in the future if careers such as those described in this book become commonplace.

A number of books have treated this subject; the brief list that follows is representative of those works.

Sellen, Betty-Carol, ed. *What else can you do with a library degree?* New York: Neal-Schuman Publishers; 1980. 350p.

> Consists of more than fifty chapters written by people with library degrees who have turned to nontraditional employment. Thirteen chapters are devoted to entrepreneurs; some chapters are written by information brokers, and others by owners of companies founded by the authors.

> Eleven chapters center on the book industry, ranging from president of a publishing firm to bookstore owner. The final group of fifteen chapters covers such areas as communications, the arts, and government. Still a useful book despite its age.

Rugge, Sue; Glossbrenner, Alfred. *The information broker's handbook.* Oakland, CA: The Rugge Group; 1992.

> Written by pioneers in the field of information brokering, this book describes the benefits of such work as well as the pitfalls. An authoritative account.

Mount, Ellis, ed. *Alternative careers in sci-tech information service.* New York: Haworth Press; 1987. 154p. (Originally issued as v. 7 no. 4 of *Science and Technology Libraries*, Summer 1987.)

Consists of seven chapters written for librarians with scientific and technical training who seek nontraditional positions. Includes information broker, translator, acquisitions editor, online database manager, and information resources manager.

Other sources of information about nontraditional careers are the organizations listed below, several of which are mentioned in the text. Readers probably will already be well acquainted with major organizations such as Special Libraries Association (SLA) and American Society for Information Science (ASIS). Other examples include:

American Marketing Association (AMA). 250 S. Wacker Drive, Ste. 200, Chicago, IL 60606. Founded 1915; 53,000 members. Publishes *Journal of Marketing* (quarterly) and other titles.

American Society of Indexers (ASI). 1700 18th St. N.W., Washington, DC. 20009. Founded 1968; 850 members. Publishes *ASI Newsletter: American Society of Indexers* (six issues per year) and other titles.

American Society of Interpreters (ASI). P.O. Box 9603, Washington, DC 20016. Founded 1965; 80 members. Publishes *American Society of Interpreters—Newsletter* (two to three issues per year).

American Translators Association (ATA). 109 Croton Ave., Ossining, NY 10562. Founded 1960; 3,500 members. Publishes *ATA Chronicle* (monthly).

Association for Computing Machinery (ACM). 1515 Broadway, New York, NY 10036. Founded 1947; 75,000 members. Publishes *Communications of the ACM* (monthly) and other titles.

Association for Information and Image Management (AIIM).1100 Wayne Ave., Ste. 1100, Silver Spring, MD 20910. Founded 1943; 8,500 members. Publishes *FYI/IM* (ten issues per year) and other titles.

Association for Information Management (AIM). 6348 Munhall Ct, P.O. Box 374, McLean, VA 22105. Founded 1978; 1,000 members. Publishes *Network* (monthly) and other titles.

Association of Independent Information Professionals (AIIP). c/o Law Library Management, 38 Bunkerhill Dr., Huntington, NY 11743. Founded 1987; 350 members. Publishes *AIIP Connections* (four issues per year).

Association of Records Managers and Administrators (ARMA INTL). 4200 Somerset, Ste. 215, Prairie Village, KS 66208. Founded 1975; 10,600 members. Publishes *Records Management Quarterly* (quarterly) and other titles.

Information Industry Association (IIA). 555 New Jersey Ave., N.W., Washington, DC 20001. Founded 1968; 800 members. Publishes *Friday Memo* (biweekly) and other titles.

National Federation of Abstracting and Indexing Services(NFAIS). 1429 Walnut St., Philadelphia, PA 19102. Founded 1958; 65 organizational members. Publishes *NFAIS Newsletter* (monthly) and other titles.

Society of American Archivists. 600 S. Federal St., Ste. 504, Chicago, IL 60605. Founded 1936; 4500 members. Publishes *The American Archivist* (quarterly) and other titles.

In the spirit of helping others, so consistently expressed by library and information professionals, the contributors to this book have generously given of their time and effort. They share their experiences simply to assist others who may be in need of broadening their horizons.

ENTREPRENEURS

ANN BEVILACQUA
FOUNDER AND PRESIDENT OF A FIRM DEVELOPING HYPERMEDIA PRODUCTS

Ann Bevilacqua is founder and president of Upper Broadway Bodega, P.O. Box 5001, Manchester, CT 06045-5001. She began her career as a high school English and art teacher. Then, upon finishing her library school training, she became an indexer at Columbia University for the Avery Index to Architectural Periodicals, promoting its use on RLIN and helping to develop databases. Next she became coordinator for library instruction at New York University. In 1989 she founded her own firm, which creates, designs, and publishes interactive software products for academic and nonprofit organizations, including hypermedia products. She has a B.A. from New College of Hofstra University, an M.L.S. from Drexel University, and an M.A. in French from Middlebury College.

INTRODUCTION

First, I'd like to discuss the founding of Upper Broadway Bodega (or, how I got into this and what bodega is). One day, as I was ripping the shrink-wrap off an early version of Microsoft Word, I heard, in the background, Paul Simon singing about the "bodegas and the lights on Upper Broadway" from the song, "Diamonds on the Soles of her Shoes." (Hum it now, if you know it, to add dramatic effect!) The initializing disk asked me to type in my name and organization. Name, that was easy; I had learned to spell it a long time ago, but organization...hmmm, a university library just didn't feel right. I wanted something else (fortissimo humming now). That's it "Upper Broadway Bodega." I was, after all, sitting in an apartment close to Amsterdam Avenue, which parallels Broadway, and it was sort of close to the upper part of Manhattan, and there were most definitely a few bodegas around. So, why not? But what does it mean? I've been explaining it to everyone from postal clerks to service technicians ever since. I call myself an electronic bodega (bodega means grocery store in Spanish) concentrating on speciality software for educational applications. Got it? (You may stop humming now.)

But that's not really how it all started. Throughout my adult life, I have been interested in teaching, which I have done in venues as a varied as an African high school, library instruction classes in a small college, and a literacy volunteer in New York. When I began to think about the career path to my present position, I felt that it was not a discernable "path" but rather a circuitous voyage. However, I have now come to realize the path to my becoming the owner of a software development company crystallized when two of my interests, namely, teaching and technology, came together in the form of my new Macintosh computer in 1987, the year HyperCard™ was "born."

As I wandered through the assorted manuals and on-screen help information, my fascination with (then newly released) HyperCard began. (Paul was probably still singing in the background.) I had some experience with programming on mainframes while at library school (mostly PL/1 and BASIC), but I couldn't figure out what HyperCard was all about. Undaunted, I explored this strange new software until its many possibilities became clear to me, and I proceeded to create many simple "stacks" (a stack is a HyperCard program).

At about the same time, the chair of the LITA '88 Conference Program Planning Committee saw one of these preliminary stacks and asked if I (along with a colleague) would be interested in developing a guide to the conference program. With much enthusiasm and little knowledge, David Lewis and I did create a HyperCard version of the conference program booklet. From a main menu, you could explore any of eight options: New user instructions, Conference program,

Who's who at the conference, Exhibits, Special events, Boston info and restaurants (an especially popular menu item), Tours, and Evaluations (see figure 1). While the programming code was crude, the idea was sublime, and I wish for a similar guide to the annual ALA Conference every time the hefty paperback version is dumped into my arms in June!

During this same period, I was coordinator of library instruction at New York University. Every semester my colleagues and I tried to teach what seemed to be endless streams of freshman composition classes. Because of the number of students participating in the Expository Writing Program (four thousand each year) and the number of part-time instructors associated with it, we were able to teach only a small percentage of these students. In trying to restructure the instruction program, development of a computer-assisted instruction (CAI) program seemed to be a likely solution. One of the main disadvantages of CAI was the lack of appropriate software for library instruction that could be definable, that is, changeable, to fit the requirements of the student's home library. The expense of such changeable programs was prohibitive, but HyperCard changed all that. Now it is relatively easy to create interactive learning modules that incorporate the advantages of CAI: the ability to simulate complex environments; encourage individualized learning; provide quick feedback; and allow student control of sequence, pacing, and even content.

I began developing several learning modules for library research that encompassed a physical orientation to the Bobst Library at NYU as well as detailed instruction on how to narrow a term paper topic and use periodical indexes and abstracts. Plans called for installing the program in the MacLab, a facility within the Expository Writing Program's offices, and directing students to it in conjunction with HyperCard stacks being developed by EWP's staff to take students through the writing process. I left NYU before that came to fruition; however, a new computer lab in the library currently holds a lab license for Research Assistant, library instruction software that stems from my earlier work.

NATURE OF THE WORK

Though the projects described above were instrumental in my conceiving Upper Broadway Bodega, the impetus for the real company occurred at the confluence of several decisions in my personal life—namely, my desire in 1989 to leave New York City and join my husband in Connecticut and our desire to start a family. We chose a living arrangement that was amenable to a home office and began the process of setting up the company.

First and foremost Upper Broadway Bodega produces, markets, and publishes interactive educational software for use in high schools, colleges, and universities. UBB also works on contract to nonprofit organizations wishing to create an interactive presentation computer program for use as a way-finding tool at professional conferences. Other opportunities exist to create training/instructional software for any organization, such as online training "manuals" or interactive retail store guide systems. Each project that I take on is, in essence, a "hand-wrought" work done on a computer. The best way to describe the product is by citing some examples.

My first project involved creating a generic library instruction module modeled after the one I began at NYU. Essentially, Research Assistant· was reworked completely until only one sequence from the original remained (see figure 2). Other titles planned are in the fields of medicine, law, business, and government information.

Another project stemmed from my experience with LITA's conference program. The American Library Association commissioned the ALA Exhibits Navigator for the 1990 Midwinter, 1990 Annual, and 1991 Midwinter conferences (see figure 3). In this large project I was one of five individuals who joined together to create an electronic "yellow pages with sounds and pictures" to the exhibition hall. For the uninitiated, ALA has approximately five hundred to seven hundred exhibitors spread over a large exhibition space. Given the size of the conference and the time constraints of those attending, the biggest problem we wanted to solve was how to connect librarians with the right exhibitor in the least amount of time. Exhibits Navigator had several access points: alphabetical listings and subject groupings of vendors, free text searching, and a graphical browse mode where the computer's mouse "walks" around the on-screen floor plan and "visits" the exhibits. (The last access point was easier on the feet but did not yield the necessary take-home freebies that a real walk does!) The ALA Exhibits Navigator, was an excellent time-saving device that was an unfortunate victim of the economic downturn. The guide's true benefactors were the exhibitors and the attendees. The national organization that sponsored it withdrew funding after the initial trial period when no outside sources of support could be found.

I also worked on a graphical informational guide to the 1991 White House Conference on Libraries and Information Services with staff from the National Commission on Libraries and Information Science. This project was conceived as a means of providing information to the conference delegates on a variety of library and information policy issues. The composition of each state's delegation consisted of professional librarians, representatives from the information industry, government officials, and private citizens. The software I had to create had to be easy enough for a non-computer-savvy person to understand and manipulate, yet the content had to be complete enough to be useful for the experienced professional. Our hypertext solution provided different levels so that users could review the information according to their level of understanding, interest, or time available.

For an annual gala fund-raising event for the New York Public Library, New York's design industry, ranging from fashion designers and artists to architectural firms, create exhibitions in the reading rooms at NYPL. During the cocktail hour, the guests browse through these exhibits. The central piece for an exhibit by the M Group was an interactive photo album gleaned from the library's collection, which I created using sound, pictures, and animation. The user clicked on one of several subject themes to initiate a computerized slide show onto overhead monitors.

Basically, all of these projects required similar steps. The first is to determine the audience for the software. Next, the content expert determines the intellectual content of the material. In some cases, such as Research Assistant. I was my own content expert. In others, I relied on the group contracting the work to provide this knowledge framework. Once the audience and the content are clear, a rough "storyboard" is created. Sometimes this storyboard need only sketch out the categories and links; other times, it must be a screen-by-screen rendering of a sequence. Since the visual impact is key, the artwork must be top-notch. The final phase of software creation entails integrating content, visual and sound (if any) material, and then writing the programming code that achieves the desired outcome. Every product needs to undergo extensive testing to guarantee trouble-free application. The testing phase requires great attention to detail and lots of time. Even a company as small as mine needs to devote time and money to research and development. I am constantly trying to improve my products and develop new ones. To this end, mine is often casting about for content experts to serve on a team to develop new products.

If the end result is a commercial product, then the manufacturing, marketing, and sales aspects of the business come to the fore. Physical packaging must be created, reviews solicited, and an advertising program developed. The order fulfillment process demands that business transaction records, inventory, accounting, billing, and shipping be kept according to standard practice. Finally, and most important, comes service to the clients. I try to maintain a happy installed base. I welcome contact with all interested parties and frequently talk customers through simple HyperTalk scripting tasks.

QUALIFICATIONS

Obviously, being a one-person hypermedia software developer takes a mix of experience, education, and just plain craziness. Prior to leaving NYU, I was invited to speak at several conferences on the creation of Research Assistant. My demonstrations of the software were greeted warmly by my fellow librarians, and I received many requests for copies. I went into the business knowing that I had at least one good program, but also feeling that I could develop others. In terms of my technical knowledge of programming, I am the first to admit that I am no Bill Gates(founder of Microsoft)! But the technology is such that you don't have to be the best programmer in the world. In a niche market, it is more important to know your audience and how to respond to its needs.

The business aspects of the business require what any new, small business requires—time, and lots of it. In setting up the business initially, I went to several workshops sponsored by the Small Business Administration. There, I gathered information and names, names, names. It's important to connect with other people who are in similar situations. I needed to identify reputable sources of other service professionals: accountants, lawyers, and, yes, even box and foam product producers. A one- person office isn't really just one person. You can't do it all yourself—seek help whenever necessary.

Because I am also the vice president for sales, it helps to have a reasonably outgoing personality. These days, most of my contacts with librarians are via phone, mail, or E-mail. Speaking engagements are a means of advertising your products and services. If telephones or microphones scare you, either take some public speaking courses or get a partner.

PROS AND CONS

One of the greatest rewards of doing what I do is the satisfaction of creating and marketing a product I designed. I truly enjoy my work. For personal reasons, I have decided to take on all the demands of a one-person shop simply because I am better able to control size and time demands if no one else is involved. I have been approached by several large library vendors who would like to buy the rights to Research Assistant. I thought long and hard on that one, but I finally decided that by retaining control over the software I could remain close to the market and in touch with the users.

I realize that this line of work is not for everyone. The current business climate means that you have to be able to live with uncertainty. Working alone means no colleagues to bounce ideas off of. My work schedule is a constant balancing act with my personal schedule. You must learn to say no and mean it. In addition, there is limited monetary gain in maintaining a small business. There are considerable start-up costs; an older, slower CPU will take its toll in your most precious commodity—your time and will not allow you to develop cutting-edge materials. Finally, a one-person office means I must do everything—accounting, billing, etc.,—and I find that I must be not only a self-starter but a self-continuer too!

On balance, for me, the pluses outweigh the minuses. The future is far from certain, but since I am currently working on porting over products to the DOS platform, I feel confident that I can continue to grow in this field for many years to come.

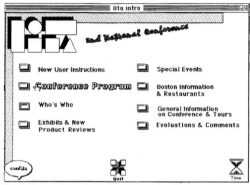

Figure 1 Library and Information Technology Association's Conference Guide (1988)

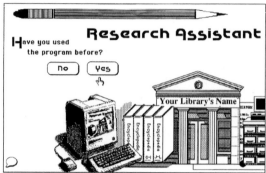

Figure 2 Research Assistant's opening screen

Figure 3 American Library Association's Exhibits Navigator

RICHARD KOLLIN
FOUNDER AND PRESIDENT
OF A FIRM PROVIDING ONLINE SEARCH SERVICES

Richard Kollin is founder and president of Searchcraft, Inc., 2246 6th St., Berkeley, CA 94710. He has founded many information-based companies, beginning in 1967 with Pandex, an index based on the technology of that period. Among the companies he subsequently founded was Information Access Corporation, featuring a computer-based file, which he and his partner sold in 1980. Following a three-year tenure as senior vice president of the Institute for Scientific Information, he created his present company, which uses a touch-tone telephone to access databases. He has a B.S. in electrical engineering from the University of Florida and an M.S. from Columbia University's School of Library Service. He was one of the co-founders of the Information Industry Association.

INTRODUCTION

It's been my experience that conceiving new products and founding companies to market these products gives me great enjoyment. Almost as soon as I was out of library school, while working as Columbia University's geoscience librarian, my spare moments were spent thinking of new products. After a couple of years there, I decided the time had come to form a company to market a microfiche-based index to periodical literature. At the time, around 1967, computers were still huge mainframe monsters, far too expensive for most libraries. My product, named Pandex, grew to become the world's largest multidisciplinary database file at the time.

In 1971 I began a six-year period as president of a small publishing company, Oliver Press, which developed thirty two reference books, all marketed by Scribner's. One of my most successful companies was Information Access Corporation, a computer-based index; my partner and I sold it to Ziff-Davis in 1980.

I then began a three-year tenure as an employee of the Institute for Scientific Information, serving as senior vice President for marketing and new product development. While I enjoyed this, by 1984 I felt the need to form Telebase Systems, Inc., a company offering a cheaper way to search certain databases. Knowing that librarians are needed to make a success of most information-based products, I saw to it that we had a real live librarian at the "help" desk all the time.

Finally in 1990 I founded my present company, Searchcraft, Inc. It is based on the use of the touch-tone telephone to access databases, with automatic delivery of data by fax, voice, or mail. As you can see, I like to mix several modes of communication if the results are effective and economical for users.

NATURE OF THE WORK

Three areas seem to have attracted entrepreneurially inclined librarians. A large number have become information brokers; many have also become involved as information distributors; and some have become database manufacturers and successful entrepreneurs.

Information brokers are everywhere. They are typically one- or two-person operations. They sell research and reference services, usually from their homes. Read Sue Rugge's book, *The Information Broker's Handbook*; it covers information brokering comprehensively. If you intend to go in this direction, study her book. Information brokers have a great national association (AIIP). Information brokering is the activity most librarians choose to start when they first leave their traditional roles.

Information distribution enterprises are involved in the hands-on, day-to-day distribution of information. Some examples of these librarian entrepreneurs are the Information Store, or Dynamic Information (document delivery enterprises), Easynet or Data Sources (online gateway enterprises).

You can always start producing a database. A great example would be Information Access Company or the Ethnic Press Index. All of these enterprises were started by librarians. Of course, make sure you haven't forgotten what you learned in school about authority control and syndetic mechanisms! If you did this activity, you would be a database manufacturer. Database manufacturing companies exist which were originated by librarians. Make sure your database is on a hot topic because you need lots of sales in order to cover the salaries of the indexers, whose jobs never end.

QUALIFICATIONS

Put simply, being an entrepreneur means setting up and running a business. It is an activity which is basically about trying to making money. Starting your own business can be intellectually rewarding, fun, psychologically rewarding. But the point is that it must be a business first. Anything other than running a business is a hobby or a philanthropic enterprise. It may be all these things, but it must be a business first and foremost!

What I'm trying to get at is, DON'T become an entrepreneur if you suspect it is immoral or if you think that it is something "nice people" don't do. If you equate making business deals with something seedy (like selling rugs in the Casbah), beware. It is an activity which is basically about trying to make a PROFIT. Neither recent library school graduates, nor seasoned special librarians who might be thinking about going into business should fantasize about themselves. It is important to know yourself and know why you want to be an entrepreneur.

Many people can appreciate intellectually the concept of PROFIT and actually be quite comfortable with the idea. You need to be one of them. If the "P" word has bad (or slightly negative) connotations for you, you should probably skip this chapter.

If you are comfortable so far, let's continue. The psychology of the whole experience is important to recognize too. Save money by doing your own psychological interview. Lie down on your own couch and ask yourself "Why am I REALLY doing this?" Take your time and answer honestly. If your answer contains the name of your spouse or a parent, Beware! It's fine to start a business to prove something to yourself (it's not only fine, it's a great motivation), but starting a business to prove something to someone else can easily muddy your objectivity and lower the quality of your business decisions.

In fact, this reminds me of several other "don'ts" having to do with your family. For example, try very hard not to borrow any start-up money from family because if you are a few days (or a few weeks!) late paying it back, it will go into the family history and be talked about for the next forty years. And forget privacy; even your little nephews and nieces will eventually hear about your late payments!

Finally the best advice of all. FROM THE BEGINNING KEEP SERIOUS BOOKS. You will need to provide them to individual investors, venture capitalists, acquisition specialists, bank loan officers, IRS auditors, and prospective partners.

Try keeping sloppy books and you will soon see what I

mean. It's hard to imagine that the cute little enterprise you are setting up today in your garage or spare room or low-budget rental space could ever grow very much, let alone transform itself into a substantial business. But, believe me, it can happen. And years later there will be hoards of auditors checking you out for everything under the sun. So start off right; be serious about your bookkeeping.

PROS AND CONS

I think I've given you an idea of the exhilaration that comes with being a successful entrepreneur. Seeing your ideas take form can be very exciting, even if you have to learn that job responsibilities don't stop when you want to take a vacation, or that keeping income above expenses is often a chancy experience. What I'm saying is, "Become an entrepreneur if you feel that you are smart enough to make a go of it and determined enough to put up with the problems en route to success. If success means a lot to you, then you won't be bothered by the hard knocks it takes to make the grade."

Lots of librarians have gone into business for themselves. Many have succeeded, many have not. This chapter is written to help your odds. Good luck!

EILEEN MACKESY
FREE-LANCE INDEXER

Eileen Mackesy is a free-lance indexer, located at 171 Cypress St., Bogota, NJ 07603. She intended to be a high school English teacher upon graduation from college. However, when she couldn't find a teaching job she went to work in 1971 for the Modern Language Association of America. During her employment she was concerned with publication of the association's *International Bibliography* for more than fifteen years. In 1988 she left to establish her own free-lance indexing service. She has a B.A. from Richmond College (CUNY) and an M.L.S. degree from St. John's University.

INTRODUCTION

Like many who graduated from college in the early '70s, I considered alternative careers because of the weak job market. Trained as a high school English teacher, I entered the market when there were few jobs and many applicants. When I could not find the kind of teaching situation I wanted, I began graduate school on a part-time basis and took a support position with the Modern Language Association of America (MLA). By 1974, my goals had changed and publishing had become my career. From 1971 to 1988, my primary focus was management and publication of the MLA's *International Bibliography* and related information activities. After managing the day-to-day business of print and online publication of the *Bibliography* for several years, it became apparent that most of my professional time was spent grappling with approaches to information access for which I was not prepared academically My professional direction and needs had changed once again. To complement my on-the-job education, I enrolled in the Library and Information Science program at St. John's University and received my M.L.S.

from St. John's in 1980.

The graduate degree did not change my life, since my career remained the same, but it did widen my horizons, provide me with new tools and approaches, and introduce me to the "information community" by giving me personal contacts that continue to be invaluable. At this time I also found that I was much less concerned with devouring the documents that came across my desk dealing with the latest theories on D. H. Lawrence and more concerned with telling people that these documents exist. Through production of the *Bibliography* and its online equivalent, I became addicted to reading indexes and working through various access problems. At the same time, I found that the administrative functions I was performing became terribly repetitive and less challenging. I decided to make a drastic change in 1988 and left the MLA to launch my own free-lance indexing service.

NATURE OF THE WORK

Considering making a change. Before making this change, I spent a good deal of time discussing the pros and cons of free-lancing with those who were already free-lancers, and I quickly developed a checklist of considerations that I had to deal with before I went any further.

Advice comes in many forms and can be enormously helpful. Advice from those already free-lancing is often on target, but must be measured against your own goals and situation. If you are planning to free-lance on a part-time basis, for instance, you will not be playing in exactly the same ball park as someone who is supporting a family of six on his or her income. Join the American Society of Indexers (ASI) and use its resources frequently. Besides gaining valuable insight into free-lance indexing, your network of professional contacts will widen immediately.

Networking, particularly, during the initial stages of starting your own business, is a necessity. Make a careful list of all the people you know who can provide you with either work or advice and spend time talking with them and listening to them. Most first assignments come from either those with whom you have worked in your previous position or friends involved in free-lance work. When free-lancers can't accept an assignment, they are often asked for a referral. Job referrals from other indexers account for a large percentage of assignments. Very successful free-lancers often find themselves overburdened and will turn to other colleagues for subcontracting—such arrangements can be very helpful throughout your indexing career.

Why free-lance indexing? Your reasons for considering free-lance indexing will affect your initial direction so consider these well. Do you have a family of six that you must support immediately? Are you a workalcoholic who cannot live without a project? Are you experimenting with indexing as sort of a second job while you are already fully employed? Is indexing something you think can be done while your children are playing in the next room? Each of these possibilities translates into different goals and inherent problems. Having to support a family of six means that you will need lots of work all the time beginning immediately, so proceed very cautiously. Workalcoholics beware—indexers are often overburdened with work (you'll love that), but can also go for long periods without a single project. Exploring indexing as a second job can be tricky and exhausting. The vision of indexing as my small children played in the next room appealed to me, but it didn't work. Be realistic about your reasons, explore the realities of your situation with someone who has already been there, and always be willing to make adjustments.

What do you require from work? Before you start out, consider what you personally require from a work experience. Are you a people person who works best in groups and requires social interaction on a daily basis? If so, you should realize that indexing itself is a solitary activity. Free-lance indexing is more solitary than indexing in an office since indexers spend most of their time with copy and computers. On the other hand, if you do not interact well with people and are hesitant about marketing your services, you will also run into difficulty obtaining jobs since marketing yourself and your services will have a direct effect on your ability to get jobs. Free-lance indexers also need a high degree of self-motivation and must have the ability to set and meet production goals. If you are accustomed to working for a company, you have also become accustomed to having any number of tasks taken care of by someone else. Be aware that you will now be photocopying, handling correspondence, billing, marketing, etc., in addition to indexing.

You should identify the focus of your business early on. Identify the areas in which you feel you will have the most success in attracting and performing work. It is better to stick to what you know best so that you can develop a reputation for excellence. It is always easier to widen your focus later, but it is difficult to recover from a poor performance on your first foray into an unknown field. Again, be prepared to be flexible. Although I had defined my focus, I was asked early on to index a project that was definitely outside of it, but the project worked out just fine, although it took a little longer than I would have liked.

Finances, of course, are probably the most important area to be considered and it is difficult to be completely realistic about this area. Since most free-lancers work out of their homes, overhead does not include office rental, but the initial costs involved in purchasing appropriate equipment, software, reference materials, stationery, etc., can be substantial. I'd suggest starting slowly—skip the fax machine until you know that you'll absolutely need one (and you probably will), but do invest in an answering machine. Areas that do not allow for skimping are indexing or word-processing software, a modem, good-quality business cards and letterhead, and membership in ASI. All of these expenses will pay for themselves very quickly. Even though you will be tempted to view your overhead as insignificant, consider and keep track of electrical, telephone, and other home/business expenses. Keep track of all of these and invest in tax assistance so that you are depreciating equipment and deducting expenses to your best advantage.

Although your business will ultimately be judged by the quality of the indexes you produce, other criteria will affect whether your clients continue to use your services. Even if you are a talented indexer with a good command of a number of disciplines, you will have to acquire a facility in a number of other administrative areas in order to succeed on your own.

Marketing is a lasting concern of all free-lance indexers. Initially, concentrating on your network of colleagues is probably the best way to go. Write to anyone and everyone you know in libraries, library education, indexing, publishing, or any other kind of business and let them know that you are now free-lancing. Be sure to specify the focus of your business. Even if these people have no work for you immediately, someone they know might and most first jobs are found through friends and former colleagues. Follow these letters up with phone calls and make certain that any free-lance indexers or consultants you know are aware that you are available for work. Although most jobs come through such contacts initially, don't sit back and wait. Continue your campaign by writing to as many publishers and companies as you can find that might be in the market for your services. Think creatively as you go about your daily life and always think indexing. A colleague of mine noted that her town's board of education always had difficulty locating policy statements, so she offered to index the board's policy book. This led to referrals to other districts. You never really know where a potential client might be lurking.

Billing is probably not anyone's favorite task. Work out a format for effective billing that is taken seriously. Use either your letterhead or a special invoice form and be sure to include a description of the service you have rendered, your social security number, the name to which the check is to be written, and when you expect payment to be made. Then be prepared to issue reminder invoices. Free-lancers seem to be on the bottom of the payment totem pole, and publishers often seriously delay invoice payments. If you have been wise enough to include a time frame for payments in your letter of agreement, indicate that on the invoice, e.g., "Payment is due within 30 days as stipulated in letter of agreement of December 2nd, 1992."

Scheduling is all-important because most of your clients will be operating on very specific and often, short schedules. If you deal mostly with writing back-of-the-book indexes, you will receive many calls with a stated schedule, e.g., we need the index in three weeks. If you deal mostly with large projects, as I do, you will often be given an ideal publication date and will be asked to provide a schedule for completion of the project. Once a schedule has been agreed upon, publishers are not happy when it is not met, even when they are at fault. I've found this to be my most difficult problem, and I still sometimes have to work many more hours than I anticipated because I've estimated my schedule inaccurately but still need to produce the index on time. In setting up a schedule, you need to have a firm sense of how much you can accomplish in a given amount of time.

When you are starting out, or dealing with a discipline new to you, it helps to actually work on fifty or so pages before providing a scheduling estimate so that you have a sense of how long the actual work is taking you. Even doing this can be deceptive, however, since the learning curve affects speed. Eventually, you will develop a good sense of how many pages you can handle in a given amount of time. Remember, however, that your time estimate must include the inevitable research time and the final editing of the index, which can often take as long, if not longer, than the initial indexing itself. It is almost impossible to estimate the time needed for a job without seeing at least a portion of the actual job. The condition of the copy (photocopy of a pasted-up page, computer printout, page density, typeface, etc.) also affect the time needed to index.

Pricing is a difficult area for all free-lancers but particularly for those just starting out. Indexers charge for their services in different ways. Some prefer charging a per manuscript page price; some charge by the hour; some charge by the number of index pages produced. ASI has conducted a survey on pricing and can provide some direction. Publishers often have their own ideas about how pricing should be formulated, but you should have a firm sense of what you require and you should communicate it to the publisher. I have found a per page price to be most advantageous, although my pricing changes, based on the density of the page and the type size.

Contracts, or letters of agreement, help keep everyone "honest" and should be written for every job. ASI has collected sample contracts from its members and can provide additional information on this area. The standard "letter of agreement" should include a description of the project and the resulting index, dates on which the publisher will deliver copy, dates on which index deliverables will be supplied, a payment schedule, a retainer request (for large jobs), a statement allowing for re-negotiating payment if the project is significantly larger or smaller than anticipated, and a date of expiration of the terms outlined in the agreement. I generally also send a sample index, based on the sample pages I've received, to the publisher with the letter of agreement.

Client satisfaction is of utmost importance to the free-lancer. Even with the best of intentions, the indexer and the client may have different perceptions of how the finished index should look. Be honest and let the client know if you believe he or she is asking for something that seems inadvisable. But remember that most indexes are works for hire and you are generally producing a product that will belong to someone else. Most publishers view free-lancers as professionals and will respect your opinion once it is explained. In the end, by paying for your services, the publisher expects to receive the product he or she considers most valuable. To encourage the publisher to think of you for future jobs, you must do your best to keep the client happy. Here again, the letter of agreement and sample index can be most valuable in setting parameters.

PROS AND CONS

Trade-offs come in many sizes, shapes, and forms. Although free-lance indexing provides flexibility, it also eliminates many of the niceties to which we grow accustomed while working for companies. Filing, copying, billing, bidding, shopping for office supplies, dealing with computer repairs are usually handled by support personnel. These functions are also not billable, so time involved in them becomes a kind of overhead expense. Consider also those previously "invisibly" paid items like health and life insurance, social security, sick and vacation time and realize that free-lancers have little control over when clients actually pay their bills. As a result, you will begin to see the many hidden costs and uncertainties involved in being on your own.

On the other hand, the ability to accept and reject projects and the flexibility of being able to develop a working style and schedule of your own outweigh the negatives for many of us.

KEVIN M. MATHEWSON
FREE-LANCE TRANSLATOR

Kevin M. Mathewson is a part-time free-lance translator living at 229 Seaman Ave., #F1, New York, NY 10034. He has worked as assistant manager of a translating agency (1986—1987) and has published translations of Spanish poetry in various magazines, such as *The New American Poetry Review*. At present he works at the New York Public Library. His hobby is designing databases. He has a B.A. in Spanish literature from Columbia College and an M.S. from Columbia University's School of Library Service.

INTRODUCTION

The first time I remember using two languages to help people communicate was in Andalucia, Spain, on a rare rainy afternoon in the mountains. A Spanish hotelkeeper was quarreling about the bill with a young English couple, who thought she was trying to steal their luggage. They had no idea she thought of their luggage as collateral for an unpaid bill. It looked as if the hotelkeeper and the young man were actually about to come to blows when I happened upon them. Both parties were speaking loudly, but neither spoke a word of the other's language. In less than a minute, by speaking a few ordinary sentences, I was able to clear up a simple misunderstanding about checkout time, and they were all laughing.

When it comes to bridging the language gap, results are not always so dramatic or so simple to achieve as in this incident. Even so, it illustrates a basic point: There are times when you simply must have a translator.

The service I offered in the hotel vestibule is actually

called *interpreting*, though many people would refer to it as *translating*. In professional terms, translation concerns only written documents, whereas interpreting refers to spoken language. Translators read and write, interpreters hear and speak. Many situations, however, call for combinations of both—"sight translating" documents at meetings (translating and reading aloud on the spot); transcribing and at the same time translating tapes; interpreting and taking dictation into another language; and so on. Many professionals work as both interpreters and translators. Both tasks draw on a thorough knowledge of at least two languages, but different skills are involved (also, interpreting usually pays more than translating). In any case, whether the languages are spoken or written, the terms *translate* and *interpret* will continue to be used interchangeably.

Under other circumstances, I might have made $70 or more for interpreting that brief exchange in the hotel. Then again, the same $70 might pay for two hours of dizzying cross-examination at a pretrial deposition full of legal terms and street slang. This underscores a fundamental aspect of both translating and interpreting: Most of the time, you can't know what to expect, so you have to try to expect anything. For a translator, this means you need the best possible library of dictionaries and glossaries at your disposal, backed up by native speakers you can consult about special problems. For an interpreter, it means you have to try as far as possible to prepare beforehand, and keep your concentration unbroken at the moment of speech.

Most of my own experience over the last fifteen years is with translation of Spanish and French documents into English, though I've also worked with Portuguese and German, as well as doing legal and business interpreting. I've done translations of poetry and prose, as well as academic, legal, and "semitechnical" translations of maritime insurance, electronics documents, and so on. I've managed teams of translators churning out huge, overnight rush jobs. I've worked part-time free-lance, and full-time at an agency. When I became a librarian, most translation faded from my life, though I continued to work with literature. Yet even nowadays, I still get free-lance work from time to time.

NATURE OF THE WORK

Anything that is written is susceptible to translation, from sonnets to balance sheets to affidavits and lab reports. Literary translation, perhaps because of its subtle problems of tone and nuance, tends to command greater prestige. On the other hand, nonliterary translation, which is everything else from banking to biology, usually commands greater fees. Generally speaking, the more technical the document, the higher the fee. This is plainly reflected in the State Department's three-tier rates for standard, semitechnical, and technical translation, which vary for each language. In terms of difficulty, different sorts of work pose different challenges. Compare a page from *Huckleberry Finn* to a page from an annual report or a lab report to get an idea of the range involved. If I were in a hurry, I'd much rather face a scientific text I wouldn't fully understand in my own language, but which would tend to break down into a one-to-one correspondence of terms, than a stream of beautiful but intricately colloquial speech. Still, even nonliterary work requires a careful ear for proper diction and, at bottom, all translation demands a deep, critical understanding of two languages.

The commonly accepted practice is for people to translate *into* their own native language from a foreign language. Thus, for me, Spanish is a *source* language, from which I translate documents into the *target* language, English. I could also say that Spanish is my *passive* language while English is *active*, though these terms apply more often to interpreting. For an explanation of these terms as used by The American Association of Language Specialists (TAALS)

and the International Association of Conference Interpreters (AIIC) see:
The Jerome Quarterly (Georgetown University). 6(1): 12; 1990 Nov/Dec.

Let's consider a hypothetical job: three days for fifty pages of legal documents from court proceedings, including tables, faxes, cross-examinations laid out in columns, correspondence, and affidavits. A complex system of pagination imposes a sequence on the miscellaneous documents. This sequence will have to be scrupulously preserved on the computer through notations and page breaks. Although the agency calls it three days, in fact, you receive the documents late Monday afternoon and must deliver the translation by Thursday morning. The source language is Spanish, the target language English. The agency is paying $600, and is charging the client considerably more. Many agencies try to exercise strict control over relations between employees and clients, including signed agreements forbidding translators to supply their own phone numbers or discuss prices with clients, and so on.

As you can see, we haven't yet translated a sentence, and already the job involves complex factors that don't have anything to do with foreign languages, including editorial and clerical precision, an ability to schedule realistically, and business judgment for dealing with the agency. For now, let's simply focus on language work.

I like to work with a minimum of three drafts. I'll start with a full reading of a photocopy of the text, flagging queries in red ink. There is a hierarchy of queries: terms I don't know at all which are clearly vital; terms I don't know which are not essential, and whose meaning I can partly infer from the context; terms I suspect may have several other meanings besides the one I know; terms I know but want to double-check; and words or expressions I'm simply curious to know more about if there's time.

If I see a lot of things I don't know, I may engage an assistant to do my query work while I turn out a fast first draft, leaving space in the text for unsolved problems. I may also invest in a special dictionary.

If at all possible, I will allow time between drafts, which helps immensely with revising. It may be lunch or a night's sleep or even a walk around the block, but a break of some kind is important.

Most of the rest of the work involves adding layers of text, filling in gaps in the first draft. By the time the last query is settled, the spelling is checked, and the document is proofread and as near as I can bring it to natural, letter-perfect English, it may have gone through six or seven drafts. Along the way, I may have relied upon an assistant bringing in answers to queries down to the last minute, special dictionaries, and phone calls to people who can unravel questions of strange idiomatic usage.

It's a different story for interpreters. As noted above, they don't have the luxury—or the nuisance—of chasing through dictionaries. Either they know it or they don't.

Interpreting conventionally is divided into three categories: simultaneous, consecutive, and summary. Simultaneous interpreting involves immediately stating in the target language what you heard a moment before in the source language. As you speak one sentence in the target language, you must at the same time be listening to the next sentence in the source language. So great is the concentration required that United Nations conference interpreters, for example, work in teams. Each interpreter is required to take a break every twenty minutes while the next interpreter takes over. It is very hard work, though it can be exhilarating. Part of the skill consists of being able to recover from slips or gaps—which are inevitable—and keep going.

Consecutive interpreters listen to a few sentences or a few paragraphs at a time, sometimes taking notes. Then the speaker pauses to give the interpreter a chance to "catch up". The speaker resumes and so it goes, back and forth. Some legal interpreting is done this way, as well as much business negotiating. It is a special challenge to be both accurate and not leave anything out. A speaker who gets carried away and forgets to stop can leave an interpreter in the dust.

Summary interpreting involves short paraphrases of longer statements, to get across the general idea of what has been said. Sometimes interpreters will have occasion to draw upon all three techniques, as circumstances vary: consecutive for cross-examination, simultaneous or summary to explain to a witness disputes between the lawyers, and so on.

QUALIFICATIONS

Let's say your French was so good in college that people sometimes thought you were born in Paris. Or suppose you grew up speaking English and Spanish or that you have a splendid reading knowledge of Russian but can barely speak a word. Can you make a living with what you know? The answer depends on too many things to allow for a simple yes or no: where you live; other kinds of expertise you have, such as a degree in biology or computer science; the business climate; international politics; and so on.

You might consider giving yourself two simple "tests" First take a look at your surroundings and note a dozen ordinary items: light fixtures, curtain rods, kitchen implements, office furniture, slatted park benches, etc. How many items could you name in a second language? How many could you spell correctly, with proper accents and capitalization? If the answer is few or none, don't be discouraged. I know many highly capable translators who would be stymied by an eggbeater or a pencil sharpener, or the wainscoting along the walls. If you're translating, you don't have to know everything at once as long as you have a good idea of where to look it up (if you're interpreting, you at least had better know how to say quickly, "the thing used to beat eggs," without breaking stride). The point of this exercise is that basic, everyday terms are the kinds of words you're likely to be using all the time. Unless you're fully bilingual, there are more gaps in your knowledge than you may expect.

Next, take a page of text in a foreign language. How long does it take for you to render it into natural, letter-perfect English? The emphasis here is on finished text. Lots of people could sketch a paragraph with rough spots in two minutes. But usually when you translate, you have to account for everything. Don't worry if it seems horrifyingly slow. It's possible to translate most of a page, and then spend more time looking for a single word or phrase than it would take to translate several more pages. When you're finished, reread your translation. Let's suppose you've understood the source text perfectly. Is your translation natural English? As you can see, sometimes with exquisite bewilderment, understanding is one thing, but being able to say it correctly in English is something else altogether.

Neither "test" is intended to measure skill or speed. Speed with accuracy and clarity only comes with a lot of practice. What you're measuring is whether this kind of problem-solving work with language interests you. If it doesn't, it's probably not worth the trouble for you to try to wrestle with translation. To my understanding, these methods, though informal, are more reliable than any strict standard, such as at least five years of schooling, at least two years of residence in another country, etc.

I count four groups of skills necessary to doing translation:

1. The foreign language skills sketched above;

2. Editorial and clerical (i.e., computer) skills to produce cleanly typed, correct documents in English;

3. Research skills for tracking down the answers to complex queries (indeed, fielding intricate questions and discovering how to solve them is basically librarian's work); and

4. Business and accounting skills for dealing with clients or agencies, managing expenses, staff, taxes, etc. To take care of the business end of things or settle research problems, you can team up with other people by working with an agency or hiring an assistant. But for the work to make sense, you must have the first two skills or be willing to develop them.

The bare minimum equipment for translating is sunlight, a good memory, pen, and paper. A reasonably well-equipped independent translator nowadays might wish to have the following:

- a computer with word-processing software for appropriate accents (even if you're translating into English, proper names and titles in the source language will require accents);

- software for interactive glossaries, dictionaries, spelling checkers;

- a fast, letter-quality printer;

- access to a good collection of dictionaries;

• a fax machine (there are agencies on the Pacific coast and elsewhere willing to work with you);

• a modem;

• an efficient local pick-up and delivery system for those documents that must be hand-delivered;

• inexpensive access to a photocopier; and

• a filing and document storage system (i.e., a file cabinet).

Various accreditation exams and certification programs are available through the federal government, the American Translator's Association (ATA), and other institutions. These are intended to guarantee a minimum standard of quality and can help you to get work, though most involve fees. Anyone interested may wish to contact the ATA for more detailed information at (914) 941-1500, FAX: (914) 941-1330, or write to the American Translator's Association, 109 Croton Avenue, Ossining, NY 10562.

PROS AND CONS

Sometimes the balance of pros and cons seems to change hourly. Briefly, they stack up as follows (bad news first):

1. The work flow is unpredictable, with slow periods interrupted by sudden high-pressure deadlines.

2. There is frequently a general lack of comprehension on the part of clients concerning the process of translating, which can lead to misunderstandings. Indeed, the unrealistic schedules cited above reflect this lack. I

remember a man who hoped to wait fifteen minutes while I did a ten-page translation; when he was told it would take longer, he asked if he could run out for a quick lunch and pick up the translation afterward. Working without distraction, I'd be lucky to finish it cleanly in a long afternoon—though an overnight wait would make it better. This kind of misunderstanding is more than an inconvenience; if clients can't understand the amount of time and work involved, they usually can't understand the rates, either. Furthermore, they are likely to show up with emergency jobs that **must be translated instantly.** Many professionals work with 25 percent to 100 percent rush surcharges for short-notice deadlines—I've sometimes done the opposite, offering special discounts for slower timetables. No matter how you try to handle it, timing is often difficult.

3. The frustration level can be high. Some things simply can't be translated adequately because they don't exist in the target language and can't be invented, and you just have to live with it. Legal terms, for example, can raise this problem. In addition, it can be disagreeable to translate documents you don't agree with at all, or consider very badly written. If, as George Orwell said, good prose is like a windowpane, translation is somewhat like a window frame. If you respect the original text, you don't have much to say about whether the window is clean or dirty or bricked-up. Finally, even if you learn to translate efficiently, the work can still be terribly slow; not only is this unremunerative and exhausting, it also tends to make you feel stupid.

4. Sometimes agencies are very slow to pay and don't pay enough. Some professionals prefer to become a regular for one agency; others work for as many agencies as they can; still others try to work only on their own account, keeping agency work to a minimum. Generally speaking, no matter how you arrange things, you don't get rich by translating.

Looking at the positive side, consider the following:

1. Translating can be interesting and fun. It offers the continuing satisfaction of problem solving and puzzle solving.

2. You can improve your understanding of your native language, while at the same time improving your understanding of another language and culture.

3.   You meet a lot of interesting people, and frequently you help them to clear up misunderstandings, or otherwise overcome the frustration of not being able to communicate.

4.   When you learn how to price things right; get the right dictionaries, hardware, and software; use time efficiently; and have a reasonable amount of work coming your way, you can make a reasonable living. Since this combination of circumstances may arise as frequently as a lunar eclipse, some people prefer to pursue translation part-time. Others, however, manage to do very well.

One hears a fair amount these days about computerized translation, which has been in development for decades. I remain skeptical. Interpreting devices of the kind used on *Star Trek,* which can instantly decipher anything, might indeed come in handy, but they are not so easy to come by. With present technology, virtually all metaphorical expressions and many idiomatic expressions are inaccessible to computers. It has been said that an early machine translation from English to Russian rendered "the spirit is willing, but the flesh is weak" to read as "the ghost is ready, but the meat is rotten."

It is true that certain kinds of technical documents rely on a closed set of expressions which can be precisely matched from one language to another, and once these correspondences have been established, the work of translation is nearly complete. Schematic diagrams of electronic circuits come to mind, for example (but even here there are problems). With most texts, however, translators must struggle to bring together smoothly terms that *don't* quite match, and they involve a special kind of wordplay beyond the ken of computers. This play is the core of translating as I know it.

No matter what happens with mechanical translation, there will continue to be a need for human translators. If you find that translating interests you, you might as well get used to mixed feelings: Sometimes it's awkward and exasperating work; at other times, you're literally right in the middle of making peace.

MARYDEE OJALA
FOUNDER AND OWNER
OF AN INFORMATION BROKERING FIRM

Marydee Ojala is head of her own company, Marydee Ojala and Associates, PO Box 770, Park City, UT 84060. She is an information broker, specializing in carrying out research projects for clients in the business and financial world. She began her career by working in several libraries, the last being the Bank of America (1979—1987), where she was assistant vice president & manager, library & information services. In 1987 she founded her firm; her title is information consultant. She continues to write monthly columns for the periodicals *Online* and *Database*. She has been active in such professional organizations as the Special Libraries Association, the Association of Independent Information Professionals, and the Information Industry Association. She continues to serve as an adjunct faculty member at the University of Missouri. She received an A.B. in English from Brown University and an M.L.S. degree from the University of Pittsburgh; she also has taken graduate courses at several universities.

INTRODUCTION

If someone asks what you do and you reply, "I'm a librarian," you are almost guaranteed that the person who asked the question has some idea of what a librarian is and does. If, however, you reply, "I'm an information broker," you can be equally assured that the person hasn't any idea of what you are and do. Even among knowledgeable information professionals, the job title "information broker" is not self-explanatory. Therefore, it's important to know just what you mean by "information broker" before you decide whether you want an alternate career as one.

Most people trace the roots of information brokering (known also as information broking in the United Kingdom) back to the early 1970s. Although the oldest information broker is probably Europe's SVP, founded in the 1930s, it is the 1971 establishment in the United States of Find/SVP (by Andrew Garvin) and Information Unlimited (by Georgia Finnegan and Sue Rugge) that defines the true beginnings of information brokering as a viable profession.

As Reva Basch notes, Finnegan and Rugge's "venture, rather than Garvin's, set the tone for what has come to be known as information broking: While Find grew and achieved stability by marketing multi-client studies and setting up 'retainer' accounts for reference services, the next wave of information entrepreneurs were, for the most part, small, privately-owned businesses that specialized in custom research, document retrieval, or both." (1)

The 1970s saw small but steady growth in the establishment of information brokerage firms. This period was characterized by a certain amount of hostility between librarians working in traditional library settings and those working independently as information brokers. Although not all librarians exhibited hostility toward information brokers, a significant number felt their collections were being "raided" by these brokers. Others felt that brokers would "steal" their clientele. As time went on, and the threats librarians thought were posed by information brokers did not materialize, relations between the two became much more collegial. Several universities even found that information brokers provided important added services for faculty and students.

In the mid-1980s enough people were pursuing information brokering careers that the need for a professional association became apparent. In 1987, some two dozen information brokers got together in Milwaukee. They spent many hours creating the framework for the Association of Independent Information Professionals (AIIP). Why not the

Association of Information Brokers? This was one of the most hotly debated items on the founders' agenda. The problem: No one could completely define the term "information broker," not even those in the profession. Also, members of the incipient organization argued that they were document delivery specialists, library developers and managers, information consultants, and subject researchers, not just information brokers. AIIP's founders decided on a less specific name for the association to accommodate the diversity of membership. Information brokers are a major component of AIIP membership, but not all AIIP members are information brokers. As a result, AIIP enjoyed a 150 percent growth rate in its first five years of existence.

NATURE OF THE WORK

Customized research-gathering information for a fee—is the heart of information brokering. You can think of an information broker as a free-lance reference librarian. It is not the best definition, but for those pursuing alternative careers to librarianship, it may be the most descriptive. According to Mick O'Leary, an information broker is "one who looks up information for you. Whether done by an individual or a large firm, whether online or conventional, it is a for-profit version of traditional library reference service."(2) Typically, information brokers are presented with research problems by their clients. They then access online databases, scan printed reference materials, and contact experts to find the answer. Notice that online databases are not the only source of information used by information brokers. Online databases are but one of many important tools used by information brokers.

One big difference between the reference librarian at the reference desk and the information broker in the office is the nature of the questions received. Ready reference questions rarely materialize during an information broker's day. Also, no one asks for a pencil, change for the photocopier, or directions to the bathroom. Another difference: information brokers' clients often want explanations of information rather than raw data. They are not content with photocopied pages from a book or a magazine article. Nor do they necessarily want a printout from a database search. They require analysis. Many information brokers find they need to write detailed reports to accompany search results. These reports outline the research procedure: databases searched, print sources examined, experts consulted. Following this outline, search results are given along with an explanation of their significance. The information broker's report is close to a market research report. It not only explains what was done to answer the question, but also indicates what these answers mean, what impact they have on the ultimate concerns of the client.

A typical day in the life of an information broker is anything but typical. Setting work priorities is a struggle. No one using an information broker's services really wants to believe the broker is working for anyone else. Yet the broker must juggle many requests from many diverse clients. Confidentiality is a must. An information broker cannot discuss one client's information request with another client. Depending on the client company, the information broker may not even be able to discuss one employee's request with another employee in the same company because it would violate the norms of that client.

If an information broker spends 50 percent of the workday actually doing research, his or her business qualifies as very successful. Information brokers are entrepreneurs, and small-business people. This means that much of their time is spent finding new clients, paying bills, sending invoices, following up on past due accounts, filling out airbills, sending faxes, keeping business records up to date, writing proposals, "cold calling" potential clients, and all the other myriad details required in running a business. An enormous amount of nonbillable time is spent simply explaining the service to potential customers. Selling any service requires customers who have a need, and are willing to pay to have that need met. Information doesn't necessarily meet those qualifications.

Furthermore, many information brokers find marketing difficult. They feel uncomfortable talking about what superb services they offer. They are even more uncomfortable about asking for money. Successful information brokers must be willing to view themselves as business people first and librarians/researchers second. They must have excellent people skills. Since many clients are phone contacts only, telephone selling skills need to be highly developed.

QUALIFICATIONS

Can you really train to be an information broker? Yes, but not in the traditional ways. Library schools rarely offer courses in information brokering, there is no certification to become an information broker, no academic degree is required. The most important qualifications are a burning desire to find answers to questions; the persistence to follow all leads; the courage to call total strangers and ask them to tell you what they know; and the capacity to sort out qualified, accurate, reliable data from spurious, biased information. In addition, a good business sense and the ability to manage a small business are keys to success as an information broker. Seminars and courses on small business management may be of more benefit to the aspiring information broker than library or information education. In the past, most information brokers sported a library degree; even those without an M.L.S. (master in library science) had library experience. But this is changing rapidly. People with backgrounds in science, marketing research, banking, law, and medicine are finding information brokering a rewarding occupation. Information brokers used to be generalists. With more information brokers on the scene, however, specialization is now common. Lawyers provide legal information, chemists search scientific and patent databases, market researchers specialize in secondary research. Library training by itself usually is not enough to start an information brokerage business. Given the lack of formal educational programs, apprenticeships would be desirable. Because most information brokers are sole proprietors, the opportunities for apprenticeships are almost nonexistent. AIIP has a mentoring committee to investigate ways of matching up new information brokers with experienced ones.

The majority of information brokers spend a great deal of time online; therefore, expertise in online searching is a must. Training offered by online hosts and database producers is essential. Reading the journals that discuss the technicalities of online searching (*Online, Database, Database Searcher*, at a minimum) and attending conferences and exhibitions such as Online (held every fall, sponsored by Online, Inc.), National Online (held every spring, sponsored by Learned Information Ltd.), and Special Libraries Association (held every June, sponsored by Special Libraries Association) is vitally important. Not only do these publications and conferences provide solid information, they allow brokers to build a network of contacts that is very useful when the need to sub-contract arises. For serious aspirants, the Rugge Group offers a seminar series on how to get started as an information broker. This daylong course is offered throughout the United States and occasionally in Europe. *The Information Broker Handbook* by Sue Rugge and Alfred Glossbrenner is an excellent introduction to the field. (3) From a Client's perspective, the most important qualification an information broker should have is the capacity to provide accurate, timely, and cost-effective information. From the broker's perspective, the most important qualification may simply be the aptitude to thrive in this type of business. Central to this is the expertise to predict the actual time involved and costs incurred in completing projects. Providing information at a loss leads to business failure.

PROS AND CONS

The decision to become an information broker requires an understanding of the advantages and drawbacks of the job. Most information brokers are self-employed. Which raises the issue of isolation, particularly for those brokers working out of their homes. AIIP has a private section on CompuServe's Working from Home Forum to help brokers overcome this isolation and discuss common concerns with peers. As self-employed individuals, information brokers must worry about errors and omissions insurance, health insurance, city licensing requirements, and copyright law, just to mention a few concerns. Information brokers should have the services of a good attorney and a good accountant readily available. They should know and understand the ethics code of AIIP, particularly as it relates to intellectual property law.

Working from home, or even from an office outside the home, requires long hours. Since brokers are not salaried, they only make money when they work. The result: Many brokers routinely work weekends and evenings, putting in fifty-to-sixty hour weeks. This is particularly true when clients are many time zones removed. If brokers want to talk with clients in Europe or Asia, they must either stay up late or get up early. Some brokers try to break into the business by having only evening hours while they work full-time at another job. This can be tricky, however, when clients want to talk during the day.

If this sounds unduly discouraging, it should be noted that there is also great fulfillment in information brokering. Self-employment allows for considerable flexibility. Information brokers can take time off in the middle of the day without having to justify it to anyone. Of course, the consequence may be working at night to make up the time.

In an information brokering business, there are no bureaucracies, no mindless meetings, no bosses to placate, no library committees to satisfy. If this makes information brokering sound like a utopian occupation, consider some of the negatives. Clients have bureaucracies, meetings, and bosses that information brokers must accommodate. It is not unusual for clients to say they need approval before contracting for services. Often that is the last thing heard from the client. Or, after a hiatus of several months, the client calls and demands the project be completed within hours.

Still, the fact that information is important and valuable is self-evident in a very capitalist fashion -- clients are willing to pay for information. There is satisfaction of really making a difference. Clients present information brokers with information problems that are vital to their business and/or their personal lives. Solving these problems can be the difference between success and failure for clients. Not only is it very important for information brokers to find the best information, brokers themselves become energized simply by the research process itself. The excitement of finding answers, the stimulation of uncovering obscure facts, the thrill of tracking down sources—this is what electrifies information brokers and makes them convinced they picked the right career.

REFERENCES

1. Basch, Reva. Trends in information broking: a view from the United States. *ASLIB Information*. 62-64; 1992 February.
2. O'Leary, Mick. The information broker: a modern profile. *Online*. 11(6):24-30; 1987 November.
3. Rugge, Sue; Glossbrenner, Alfred. *The information broker's handbook*. Oakland, CA: The Rugge Group; 1992.

CHRISTINE A. OLSON
FOUNDER AND PRINCIPAL
OF A FIRM PROVIDING MARKETING MANAGEMENT
SERVICES TO LIBRARIES AND INFORMATION
PROVIDERS

Christine A. Olson is founder and principal of Chris Olson & Associates, 857 Twin Harbor Drive, Arnold, MD 21012-1027. She was employed by government agencies and corporate libraries before serving as head of the information service for the Electromagnetic Compatibility Analysis Center (1978—1983), followed by serving as an expert consultant with the National Cancer Institute. In 1984 she created her own firm, devoted to providing marketing services for libraries and information services. She has a B.A. from Temple University, an M.L.S. degree from the University of Maryland, and the M.A.S. degree in business from Johns Hopkins University. She has written chapters for several books, publishes two newsletters, and has published a book, *Olson's Book of Library Clip Art.*

INTRODUCTION

"I want to be a librarian," said the little girl with blonde hair and blue eyes. This in response to the age-old question, "What do you want to be when you grow up?"

The year was 1959. I was in the third grade, and I had decided that I wanted to be a librarian. Twenty-two years later, after achieving my goal and working as a professional librarian in a variety of special library settings, I sought an alternative career. Winding up in my current "career" resulted from a combination of being in the right place at the right time and recognizing and taking advantage of opportunities. I am forty-something years old. I love what I do, the people I work with, and the challenges I face every day.

Marketing agrees with my personality and complements my creative abilities. Coupled with my knowledge of information management and my belief in the importance of information, my current career as a marketing consultant to librarians and information service providers is, for me, the best of all worlds. The graphics work that my firm produces for promotional materials draws upon my undergraduate degree in art history. I am able to use my M.L.S. and professional library experience to understand my clients' unique marketing requirements, and my graduate degree in business provides a solid foundation for my maturing marketing management skills. And while my background and experience just happen to complement each other (I certainly didn't plan on working with graphic designers when I was studying art history—I thought I wanted to be an art museum librarian!), I believe librarians seeking alternative careers will find the marketing profession worthy of investigation.

NATURE OF THE WORK

Like librarianship, the marketing profession is multifaceted and able to accommodate a wide range of personalities, capabilities, and interests. Most people have a limited understanding of marketing professionals' responsibilities. Although marketing has many aspects, the nature of marketing makes sales and promotion the most visible elements, causing many to draw the erroneous conclusion that if you are in marketing, you must be a salesperson. This is not unlike the belief that if you're a librarian, you must answer questions all day. Like a library, a marketing office has a whole cast of supporting players.

Marketing entails research, planning, product and service management, understanding the wants and needs of target markets, pricing strategies, getting the product or service out where the customer can purchase it, selling the product through advertising and promotion strategies, communicating to the media and being socially responsible, and coordinating all these activities into an approach that is better than the competition's. Depending on the size of the organization, a marketing office or department can be composed of one person or hundreds. While responsibilities vary according to the organization's product or service offering, certain basic marketing functions are common to marketing departments in a wide range of organizations.

Research: A well-executed marketing program includes a research function. Research can support new product introductions, identify product line extensions and positioning strategies, reveal the best promotion theme messages, and uncover information about competing products and market shares. Research can be statistically based, interactive, or secondary using existing data sources. By answering questions from your marketing department on demographic trends and competitor information, you've already been involved in the secondary research function of marketing.

Planning: Drafting a complete marketing program plan can be challenging. Unless an organization is small, its marketing plans will most likely be put together by a team of individuals, each with his or her own marketing responsibility. Planning is not a once-a-year activity, and many organizations maintain a staff to generate, monitor, and amend marketing plans (and business plans) constantly in response to external and internal conditions.

Planning can be a visionary's dream job. But those who create the plans and those who implement them have to be in agreement. Throw in budget constraints and the reality of the unexpected, and it becomes clear that planning is not for the faint of heart.

Product management: Being involved in product management implies being concerned about every characteristic of your organization's product or service. Particular attention must be paid to the product's position, both in the marketplace and relative to competing products. A product manager is always on the lookout for opportunities to spin off new products to meet demand or extend a product's life cycle as a profit generator.

You'll find working on a product line team offers a variety of assignments, with the product being the link among team members. Some of the best product managers are almost evangelistic about their particular product. Being a true believer in the product or service you manage or support makes the work easier—and less like a job.

Distribution and production: Getting the product or service into the marketplace is the ultimate challenge. Working on a distribution channel can involve coordinating activities among external suppliers, distributors, and retailers. Sophisticated logistical and negotiation skills, sprinkled with legal savvy, will carry you far in this aspect of marketing management.

Promotion: The objective of all promotion activities is to sell the product or service. Those who have a quick wit, a sharp eye, and no fear of superlatives will have the edge when it comes to pursuing a marketing promotion career. A variety of areas under the promotion umbrella may be of interest. Personal sales is one option. If you are looking for larger paychecks, this can be the best place to start. A good sales representative can usually negotiate commissions and perks—many times reaching six figures in given year. If you don't like to hustle and want a stable albeit smaller paycheck, don't get into sales promotion.

Advertising is a highly charged and stress-filled arena. Competitive advertising agencies are constantly looking for quick-witted and astute copywriters and account representatives. Agencies with international and national accounts can be found in almost city; New York's Madison Avenue is no longer the "only game in town." The pay can be generous but at the personal cost of long hours—media deadlines don't wait for anyone. Promotion also offers opportunities in exhibit management, proposal development, direct mail, advertising sales, specialty items promotion, and sports marketing.

Public relations: In many organizations the public relations function is assigned to the communications department; sometimes it is positioned within the organization so that the public relations director reports to the director of promotion and advertising. Regardless of their titles, the individuals in a public relations department are concerned with the organization's image—in its community, among its employees, and within the marketplace.

Being responsible for an organization's perceived image may include communicating with the press and planning media programs, working with members of the community in sponsoring and organizing events, monitoring the organization's visual image and any trademark infringements, training, and writing and producing communications materials for both internal and external distribution. If you have strong communication skills, and you can write in different styles, the communications department may be for you. Unfortunately, the salary may not be as high as what you are getting now, so look before you leap into public relations.

A glance at the employment opportunities section of any newspaper will reveal a wide range of marketing-related positions. Depending on the size of the organization and its industry, marketplace position, management policies, and other attributes, you will find a variety of jobs with different combinations of marketing responsibilities. You will also find that you can work for firms specializing in specific aspects of marketing—marketing research firms, advertising agencies, or public relations firms—or you can work for an organization that has its own marketing group. One-person marketing departments can be compared to one-person libraries—you do everything. Large marketing departments mean less autonomy. Look at your current library situation and determine what makes you happy—large or small bureaucracies. Whatever the answer, a similar environment can be found in the marketing profession.

Actually, as a librarian switching careers, you have two paths to an alternative career in marketing management. You can join the marketing team of a company or organization that produces or manages information services or products, or you can move to a completely different field—perhaps one that builds on a personal interest or your educational background.

Moving to an information-based organization may be the more attractive option and promises the smoothest transition—unless, of course, you don't want to see another library in your life! As more and more information products and services come to market in this blossoming "information society," more opportunities exist for marketing staff personnel and managers who have a background in information management and who can "speak the language." Publishers, online database vendors, database producers, CD-ROM producers, software developers, book dealers, furniture companies, serials vendors—they all have products based on information management strategies or they direct their products toward the library market. Your M.L.S. combined with your marketing management skills will be particularly attractive to these organizations.

Education considerations: Moving into the marketing profession can mean a whole new educational experience. In many large organizations, management positions are given to those who work their way up through the ranks. A graduate degree in marketing certainly won't hurt. If you aspire to upper management, you can groom yourself in any one of the top business school graduate programs. While there is no one "approved" program of study for a business marketing degree, if you go into public relations, being certified by the Public Relations Society of America is important. In any marketing area, you may find a degree will get you in the door, but experience and a track record will be important points in your favor when it comes to salary and perk negotiations.

QUALIFICATIONS

There are so many facets to marketing management that citing qualifications is not a simple matter. However, a few obvious strengths should be stressed.

One is a strong attraction to the world of marketing. If you look on it with a lukewarm attitude, you're apt to lose heart when you run up against strong competition or get involved in seemingly unending assignments. You must enjoy it as a way of life far different from that of the traditional librarian or it may prove to be a troubling experience for you.

Strong communications skills are very important, and creativity is essential! Research is an important part of many marketing projects, and this may be the easiest requirement for most librarians.

There are useful resources you should consult to learn more about the marketing profession. Before taking the plunge, try attending a few one-day seminars and workshops in the areas of marketing that interest you. You might consider attending night school or adult education classes to get a better grasp of what you will be getting into. Attending seminars and classes will bring you in contact with people who may be able to give you insights into the marketing profession. If you think you might want to work in marketing for an information-based organization, talk with the people who staff the exhibit booths at library conferences.

The American Marketing Association (AMA) is a good place to start your research. Attend professional marketing conferences as well as the meetings of local marketing professionals. The AMA has local chapters all over the country. Not only will you meet people at these meetings, you'll also find out where the jobs are and what salary levels you can expect. Review college marketing textbooks to learn the jargon and get a sense of what marketing management is about. Start reading professional marketing literature. You'll find a special interest journal for almost every aspect of marketing.

PROS AND CONS

The marketing profession is not without its drawbacks. For the most part you will find that the average paycheck is larger than for librarians, but performing your job while constantly keeping an eye on bottom-line profits may not agree with you. Also, remember you will be starting a whole new career, and you may have to take a pay cut to get in the door. There's probably no more job security in the marketing profession than in librarianship. If your company merges with another or your product line is phased out or your sales don't match quotas, you could be on the street.

If you don't thrive in a competitive environment, the marketing profession may not be for you. Most aspects of marketing involve competition on some level—among companies, product lines, or colleagues, or with last year's bottom line. In fact, marketing has been likened to war games and chess with its strategic moves, defensive positions, and competitor intelligence. Don't be surprised if during interviews you're asked why you want to leave the "safety of the library" for a job like this.

So what's the good news? First of all, if you switch to a marketing job, you won't be concerned about library operations anymore.

Second, if you've been in a library that hasn't gotten enough respect from upper management, you'll find the marketing function to be much more visible. And if your career objectives include assuming a CEO position, you're in luck, because most marketing departments are grooming stations for future organization leaders.

I have found that while marketing can be studied and pursued along a straight and narrow path, it helps if a person has a "knack" for marketing. Some people can "see" opportunities and create solutions; others have to follow the book. The more you are inclined toward reasonable risk taking, have an underlying confidence in your ideas, and can recognize opportunities, the better the odds that you will thrive in the marketing profession.

Marketing management may be an especially good alternative career if you are accustomed to managing your library as a business. In fact, if you have successfully switched your library to a fee-based information service, your operation is making money, and the only reason your services haven't grown more is because your organization won't let them, then you might very well be ready to leap into a marketing position where the "global village" is your oyster.

I hung out the shingle for Chris Olson & Associates in 1984. From the moment I opened the doors of my consulting practice, I positioned my firm as the marketing resource for librarians and information service producers. Before taking the leap into consulting, I investigated a variety of library and marketing career-related opportunities, from becoming an account representative for one of the top computer companies to joining an information management team of a Big Eight accounting firm. In the end I decided to give my entrepreneurial instincts a chance. Building my consulting practice into a business has brought an added dimension to my alternative career. Managing your own business—now there's a challenging alternative career. There are plenty of books and articles on the topic of starting and running your own business. There are also library seminars and groups of library consultants that you can query to learn what it's like to fire up the computer while still wearing your bedroom slippers or be up at 2 A.M. working on a client project that just won't end. But just in case you were wondering what my perspective and advice is, here it is in a nutshell: If at all possible, hit the ground running—begin your business while you still have your regular job. Unless you have a sizable nest egg to rely upon, doing without regular paychecks can be devastating. Don't impose unrealistic goals on yourself or your business. Make sure you do your marketing research homework before you begin the business.

Give yourself two years to decide whether your business is successful. Be thoroughly in love with what your business offers; you will be eating and sleeping it for the rest of your life. If you think the goal of your business is to make money, don't bother. The money will come if you offer a good product or service, but money should never be the sole reason for going into business for yourself.

Be prepared to work twelve and fourteen-hour days, seven days a week if necessary. Remember, you not only have to do client work, you have to collect the money, pay your bills, balance the budget, manage your own marketing program, make proposals to bring in more work, answer the phone, and take out the trash.

Make sure you have a strong network of friends and colleagues to call upon when the going gets tough. This is especially important in the beginning. Sitting alone in your office when you are accustomed to a working environment that includes friends and colleagues can be demoralizing.

Working at a job that you do not enjoy or look forward to is no way to spend eight hours a day, five days a week. If you are burned out, have come to realize that library work is not for you, or are looking for new opportunities, I hope this book and this chapter will help you chart a new, more satisfying course. Whatever you decide, I wish you all the best.

MURIEL REGAN
CO-FOUNDER AND PRINCIPAL
OF A FIRM OFFERING LIBRARY AND INFORMATION
CONSULTING AND PERSONNEL SERVICES

Muriel Regan is co-founder and principal of the firm of Gossage Regan Associates, Inc., 25 W. 43d St., #812, New York, NY 10036. After serving in several libraries, she became librarian at The Rockefeller Foundation. In 1980 she and Wayne Gossage founded the company which she now heads. She has a B.A. in history from Hunter College, an M.L.S. from Columbia University School of Library Service, and the M.B.A. degree in management from Pace University. Long active in the Special Libraries Association, she served two terms as treasurer (1983—1989) and was also its President (1989—1990). She has received distinguished service awards from the New York chapter of SLA and from the Columbia University School of Library Service. In addition, she has presented numerous workshops and also serves as a director of several library-related agencies.

INTRODUCTION

Library and information consulting is one of the services provided by my company, Gossage Regan Associates, Inc. My involvement with consulting, however, goes back further than the twelve years the firm has been in existence. It began with the Special Libraries Association, New York chapter, when I was asked by consultation committee chairs to act as a consultant to various organizations in the New York area that were interested in establishing special libraries. As I was then the librarian at The Rockefeller Foundation, the consultations were usually for nonprofit organizations in the humanities or social sciences that envisioned setting up information centers in their particular subject areas, making use of what was then new library technology—computers and databases. The consultations were brief, usually a half-day visit with an oral report or written outline of recommendations, and they were performed without any fee.

My introduction to library consulting was thus fairly typical, beginning as it did with SLA's pro bono consultation activities and building on my years of experience and my particular expertise, I worked with the nontechnical information center in a philanthropic organization, a library which, though small in size and staff, was very service-oriented, concentrated in subject matter, and made good use of technology to enhance its usefulness. These initial consultations were good experience for me as they showed me some of the problems as well as some of the rewards of consulting, and they started making me aware of the possibilities of a consulting carer.

When my partner, Wayne Gossage, and I established Gossage Regan Associates, Inc., in 1980 we envisioned a mix of library and information services—temporary staffing and consulting—to which we later added permanent placement and executive search. We felt confident that we could provide consulting services based on our SLA experiences, but we still read everything we could find on consulting, marketing consulting services, and pricing. Particularly useful were Herman Holtz's book on the independent consultant (1) and various writings by Alice Sizer Warner. (2) We especially took to heart Alice's very good advice to avoid going into a business that requires you to convince potential clients that they even need your product or service, before you convince them to hire you rather than a competitor. For this reason we have marketed our consulting services to those potential clients who show some interest in having a library, rather than to those who first have to be sold on having a library at all.

For other librarians, consulting may be a post-retirement career or one they undertake immediately after receiving their library or information degrees or during periods of unemployment. They come to consulting having built a reputation for expertise in some area of librarianship or information management. With their reputation disseminated through their own efforts—i.e., marketing, or through word of mouth or recommendations resulting from their writing, giving seminars, making speeches, teaching, etc.—they are eventually seen as experts, especially as experts who have the ability to share their knowledge.

NATURE OF THE WORK

A library and information consultant may be hired by a company, nonprofit organization or association, government agency, academic institution, or private individual—whoever has a problem with information management and is looking for a solution. Consulting work is found often through referrals or recommendations from organizations in the field, library school faculty, professional colleagues, or clients. We have found referrals to be more productive than directory listings, mailings, or advertising. Writing articles or books or speaking at conferences or workshops also generates consulting jobs as you become seen as an expert in some area of librarianship or information management.

Library consultants are hired for various reasons—to design or organize a new library, plan for automation, advise on space planning, suggest a cataloging scheme, develop a collection, write job descriptions, prepare a procedures manual—whatever tasks need to be done to organize or reorganize a library or improve its functioning that cannot be done by current staff because of a lack of time, objectivity, or expertise. In short, a consultant is hired to listen, observe, research, and, making use of his or her expertise, offer solutions or recommendations, usually in the form of a written report. There is frequently a hidden agenda, however, and reasons for bringing in a consultant may either be unstated or only hinted at by the client. Often these have to do with personnel. Someone has been in a position too long, he or she has not grown with the job, management has information needs to which this person is not responsive, or the organization has changed but the librarian has not. So while the consultant may be brought in ostensibly to reorganize the library, actually the librarian is the underlying focus of the consultation. A good consultant is an active listener and questioner, good at picking up on hidden agendas and balancing client needs and wishes while remaining objective and professional.

Within the parameters agreed upon when the client accepts the consultant's proposal, the consultant uses techniques such as on-site observation, interviews, surveys, questionnaires, research, information gathering from experts or vendors, or a review of documentation. The consultant determines the client's needs and the problems to be solved and then makes appropriate recommendations, with costs, time frames, and suggestions for implementation, to meet the needs and solve the problems. On occasion the consultant may be retained further to put the proposed solutions into actual practice.

QUALIFICATIONS

Whenever during your professional life you decide to move to consulting, your success as a consultant will be based on a good base of appropriate experience, education, and expertise. The education for library and information consulting will naturally be in that area, but I have also found that coursework in other fields such as computer science, management, personnel, psychology, business writing, and marketing has broadened my knowledge. It is important for a consultant to keep up-to-date with advances, new products and services, trends, technology, and current thinking in the world of librarianship and information management. This is especially true if you are not actually working in an information environment. Continuing education, attending conferences and meetings, and constant monitoring of the professional literature are effective ways of keeping current. SLA publications, annual conferences, and CE courses have been especially helpful, when they are broadened with exposure to contemporary business thinking.

It is only logical to use your own experience as the base for a consulting practice. The type of library worked in; subject area/s; the size; clientele served; whether you are a library manager, a technical services librarian, a systems specialist, bibliographer, archivist, records manager, etc., will determine the areas in which you are competent and will feel comfortable consulting. Other experience, such as designing or moving libraries, conservation and preservation, starting a new information center, automating a library, downsizing, or particular success in marketing library services, all can be used as springboards to consulting. You naturally specialize in a type of consulting according to where your interests and experience lie, and it is wise to specialize in what you do know best, rather than trying to learn on the job, keeping one step ahead of the client. After all, the client *is* paying you for what you know, not how fast you can learn, although inevitably each consultation has a somewhat different "wrinkle," which makes it a learning experience.

In addition to library and information education and experience, I have found that successful consulting makes considerable demands on other types of expertise. These include "people skills," the ability to listen and hear accurately, to empathize, and to network, thereby establishing and maintaining relationships with colleagues and professional contacts that often lead to recommendations for consulting work. The successful consultant also must be able to synthesize and think logically, be imaginatative, be organized, make good oral and written presentations, be disciplined, work well under pressure, come up with creative solutions and back them up, have sufficient self-confidence to market his or her abilities, and to be comfortable putting an appropriate price tag on those abilities. I found this requirement most difficult. The other qualities are survival skills that successful special librarians either already have or develop during their careers, but setting up an appropriate fee structure and sticking to it, or negotiating to a comfortable position, when potential clients cried poor and asked for reduced fees, did not come easy. Being service-oriented, I wanted to respond to their need for help—isn't that what we're trained to do as librarians—but that way leads to bankruptcy, insolvency, or at least a feeling of being exploited, and I learned not to fall into that trap. My rationale was that if a potential client didn't want to pay our consulting fees, which are not exorbitant, chances were that organization would not provide adequate support for a library or information center either. So developing expertise in saying no, or at least in negotiating well, was an important lesson as I began paid consulting.

PROS AND CONS

Library and information consulting is hard but rewarding work. On one hand, it is physically and emotionally draining, but, on the other, it can be a source of income and a way of ensuring that you keep up with your profession, not only intellectually but also remaining active and visible in relevant organizations. For librarians who wish to perform consultations while still being employed, finding the necessary time during working hours may be a problem; all consultations can't be scheduled during vacation. In some cases there may be opportunities within the company or organization to perform internal consultations, good experience that can be built upon later. It is crucial, of course, to ascertain your employer's attitude or policy toward employees undertaking paid consultations and to avoid any instance of, or appearance of, conflict of interest. While the occasional consultation may come the way of the casual consultant (casual in sense of time, not attitude), developing a full-time consulting practice that will provide adequate income takes both financial resources (for start-up costs and to maintain yourself while the practice develops) and time (for marketing, presentations, and proposal writing). To attempt to bring in new business while actually doing consultations requires some juggling. At Gossage Regan Associates there were two of us so that doing consulting while and at the same time lining up new consulting clients could be shared. Individual consultants have told us that this division of attention is a major problem for them, but this is true for any sole practitioner.

What is the downside of being a consultant? It can be frustrating because of the nature or outcome of some consultations. You become quite involved with the project, often actually spending more time on it than you are paid for, you write what you consider a creative, sensible, well-reasoned report; present it to the client; are thanked and paid; and then nothing happens. You will be inclined to take this lack of implementation of your recommendations personally, but the reasons for this may have nothing to do with you or your report. The organization's commitment to action or change may disappear when the cost is revealed or when the prime mover leaves (or is given different responsibilities). Or you may have a difficult client who has unrealistic expectations of what you will accomplish, or a client who shifts focus in the midst of the consultation, or who tries to influence your recommendations either subtly or sometimes not so subtly, thereby sorely trying your integrity and objectivity. Arnoudse, Ouellette, and Whalen's book has an excellent chapter on working with difficult clients. (3)

On balance, however, I believe the rewards of library and information consulting outweigh the problems. We've gained insight into a wider variety of library and information management situations than usual in an individual's work life. We've been intellectually challenged and learned a lot about organizational politics. Perhaps most rewarding, we have seen the tangible and successful results of a number of our consultations — libraries revitalized and given a new lease on life, new information centers established, cutting-edge systems put into place, new positions created, and respect heightened for special librarians and information managers and the added value they bring to their organizations.

REFERENCES

1. Holtz, Herman. *How to succeed as an independent consultant.* New York: Wiley; 1983.

2. (a) Warner, Alice Sizer. *Mind your own business.* New York: Neal-Schuman Publishers; 1987.

(b) Warner, Alice Sizer. Selling consulting services, buying consulting services. *In: Managing the electronic library.* Washington, DC: Special Libraries Association; 1983.

3. Arnoudse, Donald L.; Ouellette, L. Paul; Whalen, John D. *Consulting skills for information professionals.* Homewood, IL: Dow Jones-Irwin; 1989.

VICTOR ROSENBERG
FOUNDER AND PRESIDENT
OF A FIRM PRODUCING SOFTWARE FOR
BIBLIOGRAPHIC DATA MANAGEMENT

Victor Rosenberg is president of Personal Bibliographic Software, Inc., P.O. Box 4250, Ann Arbor, MI 48106 and associate professor of information and library studies at the University of Michigan. As a professor he conceived the idea of forming his own company to create and sell software to handle data from online searches. He has an M.S. in information science from Lehigh University and a Ph.D from the University of Chicago's Graduate Library School.

INTRODUCTION

Entrepreneurship is especially appropriate as an alternative career for librarians, because the skills that make a good librarian also make an excellent entrepreneur. The library and information fields present extraordinary opportunities for an enterprising librarian. Any consideration of alternative careers should begin by understanding that librarianship is more than a profession; it is also an industry. While the industries surrounding medicine or engineering are widely recognized, the industry that serves libraries and librarians is less well-known Just as the pharmaceutical and medical supply industries employ medical professionals, the library industry employs librarians. Working for a library — related company may or may not qualify as an alternative career, but creating a library-related company surely does.

The industry surrounding librarianship, sometimes called the information industry, is vast. The information industry encompasses all publishers who sell to libraries, producers of nonprint media, and a large segment of the computer industry. It includes all hardware and software vendors that provide access to reference information. Exhibitors at the various annual library association conferences encompass a substantial part of this industry. The great increase in the number and quality of exhibitors in recent years is an indication of the strength of the industry. The exhibits get bigger every year even as libraries face shrinking budgets and library schools face closure. The information industry can grow even if libraries do not because the companies in the industry reach out beyond libraries.

The products that the industry produces are now going to information users at all levels, from children to sophisticated professionals. That the industry is targeting those who formerly would have looked to libraries is of concern to some librarians who fear losing their value. Some librarians fear that when patrons have access to information in their homes and offices, they will no longer come to the library. But a lost opportunity to some is a gained opportunity to others. The proliferation of end-user information products will create many opportunities for alternative careers for librarians. It will create opportunities for creating the products, training users, selling information, and evaluating information systems. Creating new products and services will provide opportunities for librarians to create new businesses.

My argument is straightforward. I believe that the information industry is in the stage of growth and innovation that spawns new businesses just as the biotechnology industry does, and librarians have the skills to take advantage of the opportunities. The technical knowledge that librarians get as part of their professional training should make them aware of the exceptional opportunities in the information industry. It makes them ideal designers of new information products and services. The same training gives them many of the skills needed to start and run a new business.

At the University of Michigan, we are trying to test the hypothesis that good librarians make good entrepreneurs. We have initiated two courses related to starting and developing businesses in the information industry. Joseph Fitzsimmons, president of University Microfilms, a leader in the information industry, teaches a course on the development of information-based products and services. The students turn out high-quality work; often the projects have the potential to become the foundation for businesses or new ventures for existing businesses. Mr. Fitzsimmons has the students present their work to a group of business executives in his and asks the executives about the commercial viability of the projects.

In 1992, for the first time, I have joined with Mr. Fitzsimmons to teach a course in entrepreneurship in the information industry. This course is attractive to students, who show great skill in coming up with entrepreneurial ideas. The premise of the course is that entrepreneurship, while inherently risky, is not necessarily any more risky than getting a job. Job security, even in universities, is no longer what it was . Another premise is that the skills of the entrepreneur are just as useful in public agencies as in new businesses. The course outline is essentially the outline of a business plan. This plan includes conceiving the idea, marketing it, financing the business, analyzing the competition, developing the operational side of the business, legal issues, and "cashing out." The guest lecturers are successful entrepreneurs in the information industry, including a lawyer, a venture capitalist, and a marketing consultant. The intention is to give students some skills to start a business but, more important, the course seeks to prepare the student to seize an opportunity if it presents itself.

NATURE OF THE WORK

My experience in entrepreneurship comes from founding PBS, Inc., in 1982. I decided then that the research I was doing at the University of Michigan had commercial value. I was developing a series of microcomputer programs to download and manage bibliographic information. I was frustrated by the slow and uneven progress I was making in getting external grant funds to support my research, as well as by the low salaries paid to professors of library science. My way out was entrepreneurship. I successfully negotiated the rights to my work from the university and proceeded to incorporate Personal Bibliographic Software. I hired three students, initially part-time (later full-time), and set up shop in my attic. It was cold and drafty in the winter and hot and dry in the summer, but it was what I could afford. I negotiated a contract with a large computer company that paid the students. This initial contract plus revenue from products kept the company going for about three years. After this time, revenue alone paid the salaries. My personal investment was negligible. After ten years of effort, Personal Bibliographic Software is a solid company with a worldwide market for its products.

My training as a librarian helped greatly. I knew how to find out what I needed to know to run a business. I scoured libraries to find journals that would review or announce our products. My training gave me the insight to pay attention to details. I set up the necessary accounting and record keeping systems before a single product went out the door. Each of these tasks is a variation on setting up a database or organizing information skills of a librarian. Attention to detail is essential to a successful business. Perhaps the most important advantage I had as a librarian was knowing how to sell to librarians. The library market is ideal for the small entrepreneur, because it has very well-established channels of communication, and marketing to it is affordable. Perhaps because of the image of librarians, few outsiders enter the market.

There was no single key to the company's success, just steady effort. Over the ten years, I have learned a vast amount about topics that I never before considered important.

For example, I have learned a good deal about accounting. If I had taken a course in it, I probably would have found it boring, but it is amazing how interesting accounting becomes when the money is real and your own. I learned how to manage people and, even more important, I learned my management deficiencies. I have not abandoned the inclinations toward public service that led me into the profession. Instead, I learned that business people also contribute to the public good in many ways. I also learned that entrepreneurs have to know how to get resources without paying for them since each community has people who will gladly help an entrepreneur, especially with advice.

The entrepreneur's day is spent dealing with business professionals (lawyers, bankers, accountants, and consultants), as well employees, vendors, and customers. Starting and growing a business requires a serious commitment, especially of time. Rarely, if ever, does an entrepreneur leave his or her business at the office. Business and life blend to accommodate the long hours and hard work. Many see this commitment as negative, but my observations suggest that successful professionals in any job often show the same hard work and dedication. At least an entrepreneur has independence and the possibility of great financial reward. Much has been written about the characteristics of the successful entrepreneur, but the only common trait I have observed is a stubborn need to make things happen that often borders on the obsessive.

QUALIFICATIONS

In my experience, relatively few entrepreneurs have a business background, typically, a background unrelated to business. While it is clearly useful to understand the fundamentals of accounting, marketing, management, and operations, it is not essential. It is much more important to understand the product and the customer. The best entrepreneurs are enthusiasts who see the need for a product in their own work. They discover opportunities by seeing what is lacking in their own professional lives. One day they say, "Gee, wouldn't it be nice if we had a..." The difference between the entrepreneur and the otherwise observant person is the desire to make it happen. The entrepreneur seizes on the observation and creates the company to make the desired item. A very successful entrepreneur in Michigan was a junior high school teacher who believed that games were useful for teaching. She created her own games and eventually founded Aristoplay, a manufacturer of games. Instead of teaching, she now produces games. In my own case, I believed that it was an awful chore to create a bibliography and make it conform to a particular style sheet. I vowed to automate that process, and I did.

By stereotype or in fact, librarians have the image of being passive and more suited to public sector jobs that require little innovation. I believe this image was never accurate and it is rapidly changing. Many new librarians are innovative and are getting the skills to work effectively in competitive environments. These are the very same skills needed to become a successful entrepreneur. Librarians who are successful in developing and marketing their libraries will probably be equally successful in developing an enterprise. A librarian is trained to find, organize, and access information. These are precisely the skills that are valuable in an entrepreneur.

Starting a business requires an idea for a product or service that people will buy. This idea need not be original, but it must be proven in the marketplace. Marketing is often misunderstood. It is thought of as sales, but the two activities are very different. Successful marketing entails investigating the marketplace to determine what customers want and are willing to pay for. Marketing takes the information gathered and works with the rest of the company to see that the product is built to the customer's specification. This is what librarians are trained to do -- find out what the customer (patron) wants and provide it. In librarianship and in marketing this is neither straightforward nor easy, but success is rewarded.

The librarian also understands the nature of information products and, just as the engineer can build an innovative or better machine, the librarian can develop innovative information products and services. Information products are especially well suited to an entrepreneurial venture. If I wanted to build a new car, it would be extremely costly and difficult. At a minimum a new industrial venture requires enormous capital. By contrast, information products cost relatively little to produce and require a very small capital investment. Consider, for example, starting a newsletter or an information brokering business. In the former case, you need a computer and a mailing list. In the latter, you need to market your skills in information gathering to customers. Information businesses also can be exceptionally profitable, because once gathered and organized, the information represents an asset that can be sold repeatedly, with the only cost being to market and sell it. The information database also becomes a barrier to entry for competitors.

For University Microfilms, for example, the collection of dissertations assembled over the past fifty years is a virtual legal monopoly that could be duplicated only at great expense, if at all. It continually generates revenue as the company makes more and more copies of the same information and sells it to many customers. There are countless opportunities in the information industry and for every company the size of University Microfilms, there are many small but profitable companies that produce specialized information or information services in a particular market niche. New companies appear every year and many are successful. It is a dynamic industry that offers many options to the entrepreneur.

PROS AND CONS

Some rewards of entrepreneurship are obvious. A successful entrepreneur in the library industry can earn many times what a salaried employee can. But there is more to entrepreneurship than high salaries. In fact, the salary that the entrepreneur earns, at least initially, is often lower than he or she would earn in a more conventional job, because income goes toward the growth of the business. The building of equity ultimately provides wealth to the successful entrepreneur. The more important rewards are less tangible. While beholden to customers, stockholders, creditors, and employees, the entrepreneur is still captain of the ship. Most of us crave the independence that entrepreneurship provides. While the pursuit of wealth might be considered crass by some, especially librarians who entered the profession for idealistic reasons, the creation of jobs is a worthy public service. As a business grows it provides many jobs for the local community. I take great pride in the jobs that I have created in my community, which, for the most part, are interesting and fulfilling.

It is a common belief that entrepreneurs are gamblers and wild risk takers, and that starting a business is most often a precursor to bankruptcy. While it is true that the entrepreneur must be willing to assume some risk, often it is less than most people imagine. Often the risk is just lost income that would have been realized if the individual had gotten a conventional job. If entrepreneurs were the wild risk takers of legend, they would not succeed. A good entrepreneur is like a good investor; he or she calculates the risk and the reward and then invests both time and money accordingly. Since there is often substantial risk even in conventional jobs, the risk of starting a business might not be as great as imagined. The issue of risk often deters would-be entrepreneurs, and failure is a real factor.

Many businesses do fail, but even failure in business is

often misunderstood. Some businesses are inherently transitory, but for a short while they provide the entrepreneur with a substantial income. Others fail slowly and do not pose an extraordinary risk to the entrepreneur. Even costly failures provide the entrepreneur with excellent experience that is useful in starting another business or working in a corporation or public agency. An earlier business venture of mine failed and the experience was immensely useful in my current business. The personal loss was mostly in lost opportunities for employment during the time I was pursuing the business venture. The company quietly went out of business due to lack of sales, and neither I nor my creditors lost significant amounts of money.

I have gotten a better perspective on how hard business people work and how important they are in terms of creating jobs and innovation. I have clearly developed a new respect for "vendors" that I did not have when I was a professor of library science. The entrepreneur's work is varied, difficult, and a constant learning experience. I know of no career where the work varies more from day to day. The challenges of starting a company are different from those of running one. At the start of a business, the entrepreneur does everything from raise money to clean the office. All of the entrepreneur's skills are used, and other skills are begged, borrowed, or bought. The reward of starting a business is much more than financial. It is not unlike a very broad university education. You quickly learn to develop products, manage people and money, sell, and market. As the enterprise grows, you need new skills. A growing organization needs management. It must be structured, and the structure must change to accommodate new employees and new functions.

Entrepreneurship is an exciting option for the adventurous librarian. I can think of no other career that offers as much stimulation and satisfaction. The information industry is filled with successful entrepreneurs and many are librarians.

SUE RUGGE
(WITH CINDY GULLIKSON)
FOUNDER AND PRINCIPAL OF A COALITION OF
INDEPENDENT INFORMATION BROKERING FIRMS

Sue Rugge, widely recognized as the "first information broker," is currently principal of the Information Professionals' Institute, 46 Hiller Drive, Oakland, CA 94611. IPI offers seminars in both the business and research sides of fee-based information-gathering services. She worked in and eventually ran corporate libraries in the electronic and aerospace industries from 1962 to 1971. Her career in information brokering began when she cofounded Information Unlimited in 1971, which provided both research and document delivery services for the business and science technology communities. She went on to found Information on Demand in 1978, a company she built from scratch into a leader in the information field, with annual sales of 2 million. After selling IOD, she founded The Rugge Group, a coalition of independent information professionals, which offers primary and secondary research services. She has recently sold it to Jim Hydock, who is now managing director. Sue is a past president of the Association of Independent Information Professionals and has been a member of SLA since 1968. With more than thirty years in the information field, Sue has a lifetime of experience and expertise to share.

Cindy Gullikson earned an M.L.S. from San Jose State University and is currently director of operations of The Rugge Group.

INTRODUCTION

Right off, I want to make sure you don't look upon me as a visionary. While many people have dubbed me the "mother of information brokering" or even the "grandmother," I never sat down to fashion an industry. I think of myself as a survivor, not an innovator, although I grant you that one needs to be innovative to survive.

My library career started in 1962 when I was hired by General Motors Defense Research Laboratories as a typist. I was assigned to the library to type catalog cards and interlibrary loan slips (now you know why I said grandmother!). If I had been assigned to the insurance pool or the engineering department, I would not be sitting here writing this chapter. However, there I was, in the library. I spent the next three years learning everything I could about research. When I left that library and headed back to the San Francisco Bay area where I was born, I decided to try to get a job in a corporate library. All you degreed librarians reading this must be horrified at my brashness, but in fact, in those days, most self-respecting librarians were working in academia or the public sector. Thus it was not impossible to call yourself a librarian and still apply for a corporate position. I did just that at Physics International and was told that as long as I passed the typing test, I could have the job and set up the library in my "spare" time. I accepted the position. From there I went on to run the libraries at Dalmo Victor and Singer Business Machines (Friden Calculator Co.). In 1971, after Singer bought Friden and ran it into bankruptcy, I found myself out on the street unemployed.

In 1971 we had as bad a recession, especially in California, as we are experiencing in 1992. Here I was with no college credits of any kind in competing with hundreds of degreed librarians who were also out of work. I was a widow with two children; how would I make a living? Was I doomed to go back to the typing pool whence I had come? No, I decided, that was not for me. I thought if I could find five companies that would hire me to do research one day a week, that would constitute a job. So I went in search of those five companies, which in the long run proved to be elusive.

While searching, I met a real librarian named Georgia Mulligan (she is now Georgia Finnigan, owner and president of the Information Store). She liked the idea of working for people on a project basis where she would have enough time to do all the research that was needed. We decided to become partners we just shook hands and said, "We are now partners." We named our company Information Unlimited. She continued to work at Shell Development, and I started to pound the pavement looking for our five companies. We never did find anyone who was willing to commit to a specified amount of time. But, in our quest, we let many, many people know we were available for research projects.

Eventually people started to call and ask for a copy of this article or that military specification or patent. It wasn't research, but it was a start. About the same time on the east coast, Andy Garvin and Kit Bingham were busy writing their business plan for what would be known as FIND/SVP. Information Unlimited and FIND/SVP were the start of the information brokering industry as we know it today.

NATURE OF THE WORK

What do information brokers do? There are as many answers to that question as there are brokers. Generically, we gather information to help our clients solve problems. Our work is done on a custom basis, so each time the phone rings, we are basically starting over. Sure, we gain more experience with each project, but no two projects are ever the same. There is no opportunity to take advantage of the industrial revolution's concept of replication. That is why it so difficult to make money in this business.

Some information brokers only do online searching, while others concentrate on manual research on the telephone or in libraries. Many brokers specialize in areas such as patent work, competitive intelligence, econometrics, medicine, import/export, biotech, pharmacology, market research, and demographics. Some, like The Rugge Group, use a combination of online and telephone work. (Our split is about fifty-fifty.)   Some brokers only gather the information; others analyze it and draw conclusions. The latter group is more fortunate. They can call themselves consultants and, therefore, charge more for their services. There are also brokers who do only document delivery. They provide copies of specific material where the client has the bibliographic reference but not access to the full text of the document.

The vast majority of information brokers are sole practitioners, and they have the roughest time. Firms like The Rugge Group, InfoLink, Cooper Heller, Burwell Enterprises, and FIND/SVP, which have multiple employees, stand a better chance. It is very difficult to be the marketer, researcher, and bill collector all rolled into one. You will get established faster, that is, create that critical mass of a client base, if you can devote your first year to marketing. Think about subcontracting the work you get in the beginning to an established broker. You will accomplish several things: You will have more time to devote to marketing; You will learn how established brokers quote and set budgets; and You will see what tools they use and how they go about doing the work in the most thorough, cost effective manner. By subcontracting, you will know what your expenses are up front. You can also feel confident that those first few projects are going to serve you well as references in the future because they were done by experienced people. If you are saying, "but I want to do the research," you are not thinking like a successful businessperson.

A Day in the Life of an Information Broker

What is a typical day in the life of an information broker? Of course it depends somewhat on how long you have been in business. But here's a taste:

The phone is ringing as you open the door. The attorney says, "I just got wind of a surprise expert witness on the other side. Who is he? What has he written? Where has he worked? Where did he go to school? Has he ever testified as an expert witness before? I have to go. I'll call you at the eleven o'clock recess for the answers." If you are lucky, he didn't say, "and don't spend more than $200 finding the answers."

You start to go online to do an author search and the phone rings again. It is Jane Doe from Florida who is thinking about being an information broker. "What is it like? How much money can I make the first year? What kind of computer should I buy?" While I get a disproportionate number of these calls because of my reputation, these questions are asked of many of my colleagues as well. Anyone who has stayed in business for more than a couple of years can regale you with stories about these calls. You tactfully explain that you are on deadline and would be glad to give the caller a few minutes tomorrow.

Back to the computer. The witness in question is a doctor named James Elroy. That shouldn't be too hard. It sounds fairly unique. BUT, there are one hundred hits by J. Elroy. As you scroll through titles, you realize there has to be more than one. Looks like one is a gynecologist, one a urologist, and one an oncologist. The attorney didn't say what the case was about or what this person was supposed to be an expert in. Now what? You call his secretary; does she know anything about the case, you ask. You get some helpful hints and decide to go with the urologist. Where is he now? The most recent citation is from 1989. The hospital says he doesn't work there anymore. You call personnel.

Your other line starts ringing. "Where is my Federal Express package? You said I would have it by 10:30." You look at your watch; it can't be 10:30 already. You tell your client on the phone you will call Fed Ex and get back to her ASAP. Back to the hospital personnel office. They give you a lead as to his current whereabouts. You decide to take a chance and ask if they happen to have his CV? Yes (wow, did you luck out). "Could you please fax it to me?" you kindly ask. "Well, I'm not sure; that may be against company policy." You plead a little more, "All I really need is a list of his publications and where he went to school. My boss will be really unhappy if I can't get this. PLEASE."

It is 10:45, the phone rings again. "Oh, Ms. Campbell, are you ready to go on that project we discussed last month. Of course I'll will be happy to discuss the details. May I call you back after lunch? What, you're leaving for vacation at noon and want to get this project off the ground? Well of course, let's discuss it right now." With that crisis averted, you finish off the search for Dr. Elroy and are ready for the attorney's phone call.

You spend the next several hours putting the polishing touches on a market study of the horse leg-wrap and blanket industry and get it ready for Federal Express. That reminds you to call your client with the delayed package. At three o'clock she says she got the package at eleven, but hasn't opened it yet. You begin on a stack of follow-up calls to potential clients as well as marketing letters and brochures, but you decide you've procrastinated long enough on tomorrow evening's SLA talk. You're just in the middle of a particularly witty thought when the phone rings another rush project. This one you subcontract to your colleague with the international finance background. With the day nearing an end, you pack up your evening's reading material —
Information Today, Chronolog, Online, Business Week, and

The Wall Street Journal and head home.

The scenario above is not an unusual day in the life of an information broker. I could describe a few more, but that might take up the rest of the space in this book. Suffice it to say, the days can be hectic, challenging, frustrating, disappointing, ecstatic, *and* never-ending.

QUALIFICATIONS

So you've been a librarian all your life, or you just got your M.L.S. Maybe you are a market researcher or an investigative journalist. Or maybe you just love books, or you've always considered yourself an information junkie. Maybe you just got your CompuServe password and discovered a whole new world of information-gathering capabilities or you are a programmer or systems analyst, so this online stuff will be easy for you. You say you're tired of working for someone else or you were just laid off or maybe you are about to retire? What are you going to do next?

"I know," you say, "I'll become an information broker. All I need is a computer and I can work out of my home. It's a cinch; why I bet I can make $50,000 to 75,000 just for starters. After all, this is the information age, isn't it?"

The above are just a few of the scenarios I hear every day from aspiring information brokers. When I hear, "Do you realize what a gold mine you're sitting on?," I think to myself well, I've been sitting on it for twenty years and it hasn't hatched yet! Or when the first question is, "What kind of computer should I buy?" or "Which vendor system should I subscribe to?," I know the caller is not thinking the way a potentially successful broker does.

The first and most important question you should ask yourself is, *Do I like to sell and who am I going to sell to?*

"Oh," you say, "everyone needs information. The whole world is my market. I'm a generalist. Clients won't be a problem, but I have to get set up first, get up to speed on these databases, get my software in order..." "No," I respond, "you have to try your hand at selling because if you can't sell, you won't have a business. Information services are hard to sell."

Keep in mind the importance of marketing. To help you figure out your potential market niche, ask yourself these questions: Whom do I know and what do I know? Is there a match there? What have I done that has established my credibility with some group? What client bases have I served? Do my patrons feel connected to me personally? If I have been a salesperson, can I transfer my client base to an information brokering potential base? To what professional groups do I belong, e.g., executives, engineers, chemists, CPA or small-business owners? What subject expertise do I have? What types of industry are in my geographical area? What types of people do I feel comfortable with?

Capitalize on who you are and what you have done before. Did you discover an information need in your former job that would lend itself to your new services? Can you provide an information solution to some of the problems your former department faced? You must either have a niche of clients in a particular industry or specialize in a field that will draw a variety of types of clients. If you are a corporate librarian, do you see an opportunity to provide more in-depth services than you are currently able to offer? As an independent, perhaps you can do that full-blown market study that Ms. Smith in Marketing needs but can't get from the library due to a shortage of staff and funds.

Education: I would be a hypocrite if I said you have to have an M.L.S. But, if you're going to try to make it by yourself, you do need some type of information resource background, and the M.L.S. degree is the one most commonly held. You can't sell the service if you are not aware of the resources. However, as I said before, it is very difficult to make it as a one-person operation. So if you have a business/marketing background, team up with someone with an information resource background.

When and if you decided to get an M.L.S., you were at a cross-roads. Most of you who chose to go for an M.L.S., did so for similar reasons. You liked the atmosphere in which you would work. Of course you loved books and the intellectual challenge, but you chose to put it to work within a relatively "safe" environment. The fast track corporate world was not for you. Well, if you want to be a successful information broker, you *are* in the fast lane. If you don't like that, you need to think about having a partner or hiring an outgoing marketing type who does. It is a given that if you don't like what you are doing, you won't be good at it.

Traits of a successful information broker: In my seminar The Information Broker's Seminar which discusses all the business aspects of information brokering, I speak of the traits of a successful information broker. They are the ability: To sell yourself and therefore your service, to handle rejection, to manage a business, and, finally, to access information sources using well-developed information skills and subject expertise. These traits are different from those of a good online searcher. Successful online searchers need a logical, analytical mind, excellent communication skills, enthusiasm, curiosity, self-confidence, and decision-making skills. All of the above will propel you in the direction of a successful information broker, but if you are uncomfortable selling yourself, you will never have the opportunity to put the rest of your traits into practice.

PROS AND CONS

There are many pros. You are your own boss. You

work your own hours. You decide how you are going to approach the problem. You choose your clients, subcontractors, and employees. You derive a great deal of satisfaction from helping people. You are intellectually challenged every day. You have the opportunity to do online searching (if you like it not everyone does). You can work out of your home. You can decide when you want to work (this isn't really true, but it sounds good).

Now for the cons. If you work by yourself, it can be lonely. The pressure is immense. The work never stops. There is the administrative paperwork, invoices to be sent out, bills to be paid, and collections to keep current. If you take a vacation, you stop earning money. You pay self-employment taxes twice what you would pay if you were employed. There are no medical benefits, no retirement, no sick leave or paid vacation. The buck always stops with you. You get tired of spending your evenings with rubber chicken at the Chamber of Commerce, and other meetings.

Despite what I said earlier, you can't really work your own hours. You have to be available when businesses are operating. It is very difficult to work only part-time or in the evenings. Clients usually want results quickly, and if they call and get your machine, they may not call again. While some of the research may be performed during off-hours, such as online searching, your marketing efforts must take place during normal working hours.

On the other hand, if you have employees, you have all the responsibilities that go with being an employer. I want to reiterate here that I don't think you can really grow a business without help, but with employees come responsibilities. They get paid whether you do or not. They give their all, we hope, but they expect security in return. Think about what you expected when you were employed. They will want that too, and since you are only one person, they are going to be worried about job security. I know with all my heart that I never could have made Information on Demand into a 2 million dollar company if it hadn't been for my employees. However, the main reason I decided to sell it was that I couldn't stand the pressure of fifty people depending on me for their livelihood. To me, that was a huge responsibility. I think our country would be better off if other CEOs felt the same. But I am speaking to you as a colleague, not as an M.B.A. professor. I have the utmost respect for my fellow AIIP (Association of Independent Information Professionals) colleagues. They know what it is like to lay themselves on the line, both for their clients and for their employees. It is tough, *but* it is worth it if this challenge appeals to you.

Competition: If you decide to try it, remember, we will not be competitors--we are resources for each other. Many people have questioned the wisdom of my giving seminars on information brokering because they fear that I am training our competitors. However, our main competitor is ignorance. Prospective clients will not ask you to do projects if they have no inkling of how they can be done. So educating the marketplace to the tools and resources that are available to us becomes a major issue for growing your business and our industry. The more people we have *responsibly* marketing and educating, the faster we will reach the critical mass known as an industry. Right now there are only three hundred full members of AIIP. That is hardly enough to be considered an industry. There is still plenty of room out there for more brokers. So I will say again, think of your fellow entrepreneurs/intrapreneurs as resources, not competitors. Good luck. Let me know if I can help.

GUY ST.CLAIR
FOUNDER AND PRESIDENT
OF A FIRM OFFERING LIBRARY AND INFORMATION
SERVICES

Guy St. Clair is founder and president of OPL Resources, Ltd., and St. Clair Management Resources, 1701 Sixteenth St., N.W., #644, Washington, DC 20009. He began his library career at the Library of Congress in 1960-61, followed by employment in three university libraries and a public library. He served as library director at The University Club of New York from 1979 to 1987. In 1984 he founded OPL Resources, Ltd., later publishing the first issue of *The One-Person Library: A Newsletter for Librarians and Management* in 1984. He has an A.B. from the University of Virginia and an M.S.L.S. from the University of Illinois. He has been active in library associations, including serving as president of the Special Libraries Association (1991-1992), and the SLA's New York chapter (1989-1990), and recipient of the SLA Professional Award in 1989. He has written and lectured extensively on librarianship and information services and has conducted numerous workshops.

INTRODUCTION

An entrepreneur is defined as one who assumes the risk and management of business; that person is seen as a contractor, as it were, an organizer of business, trade, or services. Certainly such a definition is appropriate to describe what I do for a living.

I doubt if my experience is very unusual. For those who have chosen careers in library and information services, there seems to be an amazing array of opportunities for what I choose to call "entrepreneurial" librarianship. Much of what the information worker does is already (or can be) entrepreneurial in practice, and in fact I wasn't long into my career as a librarian before I realized that I was practicing "entrepreneurial" librarianship. Of course, we didn't call it that in those days, and had I thought about it in those terms, I might not have been very interested in the idea, but in fact entrepreneurial librarianship was what I was doing.

Entrepreneurial librarianship requires the same qualities that entrepreneurial business requires: a willingness to take risks, organizational skills that lead to the successful resolution of the customers' (that is, the library's patrons') problems and attention to their needs, and, probably more than anything else, a desire to perform as if the venture must succeed or the practitioner won't be paid.

Entrepreneurial librarianship is librarianship that provides library and information services from the point of view of the user, a point of view which Michael Gorman defines in the user's basic question: Are the services and materials available to me when I need them? (1) And the success of library and information services, in entrepreneurial terms, is not measured in assets, in numbers of volumes, or in a count of reference questions answered, but is determined, in David Penniman's terms, in a "measured-value approach.... Resources required are quantified but so is output, and productivity is measured." (2)

Of course, for all librarians and information service professionals, service is basic, and as a young librarian, like all my fellow graduates, I approached my work with the goal of service, for that was why I had gone into the profession in the first place. Librarianship has always been a career in which practitioners serve others, and the idea of being of service in an intellectual environment, of sharing a natural interest in the pursuit of intellectual objectives with colleagues and readers and at the same time being of service to them, was an idea that had much appeal to those of us who came of age professionally in the early 1960s.

Yet much to the dismay of some of my early supervisors, I seemed to bring to the service idea some of the qualities that I now recognize as entrepreneurial: I was always asking "Why?" I was anxious to take (calculated) risks, I had little or no patience with the bureaucracy and the red tape that goes along with it, and I was particularly charmed by the prospect of performing a service and being appreciated for having performed it (or, if not thanked literally, at least having the satisfaction that I had given the patron what he or she had come to me for).

More than anything else, however, I recognized in my early career that although I was not in a position to make the decisions that would enable me to succeed, I was nevertheless expected to perform in such a way that success would follow. In other words, I had to answer to somebody else, and if there is any single attribute that characterizes the entrepreneurial mind, it is that the person wants to be in charge. The entrepreneur wants to make the decisions and is willing to accept the responsibility for making the decisions that lead to the successful conclusion of any transaction or endeavor. It was that maverick spirit (or independent spirit, if you wish) which led me to conclude that I should be working for myself, or at least be in charge of my own company.

About ten years into my professional career, after holding several library positions, I found myself working in what was called, in those days, a "one-man" library. Finding little in the literature about the specific needs of employees in these libraries (which I chose to call "one-person" libraries), I found that I was writing articles and leading discussions at library conferences, and that there was a considerable amount of interest in the subject. As it happened, I changed positions, leaving the only one-person library job I had in my career, and I became the director of a large private library, with a charge to build staff, automate, raise funds, and generally revive what was, at that point, a moribund library and information service. At the same time, I continued to get requests for further writing, consulting projects, and workshop programs on the subject of one-person librarianship, and it soon became apparent that I could have a dandy little "second" career if I chose to do so. And serendipity played its part, for as it turned out, the person whom I hired to be the second in command at this library was a young man with the enthusiasm, intelligence, and energy to do not only what he was supposed to do for our work, but to encourage me to do other things as well. Thus it was that after several years of working together, Andrew Berner and I decided to use our own time (and absolutely and conscientiously apart from our duties at our place of employment, for neither of us was interested in any conflict-of-interest problems) and our own resources to take advantage of the market we found. We decided to publish a newsletter for librarians who worked alone.

In January 1984 OPL Resources, Ltd., was organized and in May 1984 the first issue of *The One-Person Library: A Newsletter for Librarians and Management* was published. It was successful. We went on to offer seminars and consulting advice to clients who were willing to use us on weekends or when we could take vacation days from work, and, with the publication of a book on one-person librarianship (which I wrote with Joan Williamson, a professional colleague from the United Kingdom), our path was set. By 1987, I had determined that this version of entrepreneurial librarianship could work in the open marketplace, and I resigned my position to devote all of my efforts to our business.

NATURE OF THE WORK

OPL Resources, Ltd., is a publishing, training, and management consulting firm specializing in services for the minimal-staff library and information community. It is an independent company with offices in New York and

Washington, D.C. The company has three divisions. OPL Publishing provides newsletters and special reports for the library profession, and the company's best-known product is *The One-Person Library: A Newsletter for Librarians and Management.* The OPL Consultancy provides management consulting services for special libraries and information agencies, offering technical and management advice. The firm specializes in such areas as strategic planning, organizational behavior, information and organizational audits, management communication, financial planning, development of advocacy and support groups, and marketing of library and information services. OPL Training provides seminars, workshops, speakers, and continuing education courses for the library and information services community, and the company organizes in-house educational and professional development courses for a variety of corporate clients and library and information service professional associations. Custom programs are frequently designed for specific clients.

In June 1992 we formed a second company to provide what we like to characterize as quality management support to the broader-based library and information services community. Much of the work of OPL Resources, Ltd., was being sought beyond the one-person library market, and it seemed appropriate to offer a corporate entity through which these services could be channeled as well. St. Clair Management Resources has as its mission the provision of any service that assists others in the organization of information and the management of information services. This company, too, has provides services similar to those of OPL Resources, Ltd. The SMR Consultancy offers collection evaluation and enhancement programs, personnel training (particularly in such areas as customer service improvement programs and management leadership programs), and creation and implementation of financial support and development programs. In addition, St. Clair Management Resources includes SMR International, the company's advisory, marketing, and distribution arm. With contacts in several parts of the world, SMR International provides a variety of connections and introduces clients to one another. SMR International's services are used by companies seeking to learn more about the international library and information services marketplace, and SMR International is engaged by American, Canadian, European and Australian clients for data-gathering projects, market studies, executive search, and other activities related to library and information services in the international area.

QUALIFICATIONS

Success as an entrepreneur in library and information services requires several basic educational qualifications, all of which are (or should be) required for success in the library and information field anyway. These are a strong undergraduate education, a graduate degree in library and information studies, and substantive continuing education and professional development . Some entrepreneurs will need the discipline of a graduate degree in business administration, and others will read and participate in lifelong learning programs to approximate the educational requirements they would have achieved with a graduate business degree. For the type of work I do, you must be comfortable with selling; marketing of any entrepreneurial activity is basic, and if you are uncomfortable promoting what you can do, you should steer away from this kind of activity.

In order to publish successfully, you must be comfortable with writing and editing, and the persuasive skills required for finding materials and encouraging others to write for your publications are always part of the picture. Consulting requires an ability to meet with a client (and his or her managers), to listen to their descriptions of what concerns them, and then, in nonthreatening terms, analyze what is needed to correct or enhance the situation. Consulting also requires negotiating skills, not only with clients, but with other consultants whom you will hire to work with you in those areas where you are not particularly strong. Thus, the ability to get along with others, to work together to achieve mutually agreed-upon goals, is required, and the ability to see a colleague as one who strengthens your skills, rather than as a competitor who will take something away, is important.

Training requires slightly different skills. Of course, you must be a good businessperson and be able to negotiate fees and time demands and the like, but equally important is what I choose to call the "comfort" factor. If you are a good trainer, you are comfortable on your feet and don't mind standing in front of a roomful of people whose attention all day long is going to be riveted on you. You have to prepare well, of course, and each seminar includes as much preparation time as presentation time. But the true test comes when you are in front of the group and are expected to impart knowledge, facilitate the discussion, and enable participants to leave with the feeling that they've learned something new. Self-confidence and solid communications skills are essential.

Finally, managerial skills are basic. While most entrepreneurial activities start small (often with a single-person operation: the entrepreneur and a telephone), success leads to growth and office staff soon becomes part of the picture. You must be a good supervisor, in delegating the day-to-day activities and planning the company's work, and you must be a manager, planning for the future and seeing that the company stays on the course. Management skills, practiced every day, are fundamental for the entrepreneur, and regardless of how much he or she is in or out of the office, the role of manager cannot be dismissed lightly if the company is to succeed.

PROS AND CONS

In discussing any topic as subjective as entrepreneurial

librarianship, the advantages and disadvantages of the work are necessarily based on your personal interests. The disadvantages are all too obvious. When there's a recession, when you are distracted by personal or other professional obligations, or when you are simply too overextended to devote attention to marketing and promotion the services, business will fall off. The ventures (defined solely in terms of the venture's profit and loss statement at the end of the year) is directly related to the amount of time and energy the entrepreneur is able and willing to provide, and the temptation to engage in activities that are not related to your work can be a powerful barrier to overcome. Nevertheless, the connection is so direct, and the results so predictable, that the entrepreneur is careless only once or twice before realizing that every business decision must be based on answering one question: "What will this mean for the company?"

I hope that the advantages of entrepreneurial ventures have been an underlying theme of this essay. The pleasures of being directly responsible for customer satisfaction, the constant interactions with customers, the opportunities to play a part in the advancement and enhancement of the library and information services profession, the opportunities for service, and, not least of all, being paid to do what you like to do, are all advantages that attract me to the entrepreneurial role.

Despite the problems that come along (and there are problems), being in charge of your own success is a very powerful paradigm. And success, however it is defined, enables you to do what you want. In the final analysis, our role in the library and information services profession is ultimately determined by how we feel we can contribute to the profession. For some of us, entrepreneurial librarianship is the best way to make that contribution.

REFERENCES

1. Gorman, Michael. Laying siege to the fortress library: a vibrant technological web connecting resources and users will spell its end. *American Libraries.* 17(5): 325-328; 1986.

2. Penniman, W. David. *Preparing for Future Information Delivery Systems, the Second Annual John T. Corrigan Memorial Lecture, May 3, 1991.* Washington, DC: 1991, The Council of National Library and Information Associations(CNLIA), Occasional Paper No. 2, pp. 7-8.

PATRICIA GLASS SCHUMAN
PRESIDENT OF A PUBLISHING COMPANY
CONCENTRATING ON BOOKS BY AND FOR
LIBRARIANS

Patricia Glass Schuman is president of Neal-Schuman
Publishers, Inc., 100 Varick St., New York, NY 10013.
Neal-Schuman publishes books and journals for librarians.
Prior to co-founding Neal-Schuman with vice president Jack
Neal in 1976, she was senior acquisitions editor, Book
Division, of R.R. Bowker Company. She has also served as
associate editor of *School Library Journal*, Acquisitions
Librarian at New York Technical College; teacher of library,
Brandeis High School; and Librarian Trainee, Brooklyn
Public Library. Ms. Schuman has been a visiting lecturer at
several library schools and a consultant, and has written
scores of articles and several books. An active participant in
professional organizations, she served as treasurer (1984-
1988) and president (1991-1992) of the American Library
Association and has been a member of the board of SLA's
Library Management division. Ms. Schuman has won many
awards, including the Distinguished Alumni award from
Columbia University's School of Library Service and the
SLA Publishing Division's Fannie Simon Award for a
distinguished contribution to publishing and librarianship. Ms.
Schuman holds an A.B. from the University of Cincinnati and
the M.S. from Columbia University's School of Library
Service.

INTRODUCTION

I probably owe my success in publishing to the fact
that, when I graduated from college, I didn't know how to
type. As a college graduate with an English major, my dream
was to work in publishing. Though I kidded my parents about

opening an English store, in reality I was one of thousands of young women in New York competing for low-level editorial secretary or assistant positions. With few typing skills, I was not in great demand.

Frankly, I had never even considered entering the library profession until after I answered a blind advertisement in the *New York Times* for "college graduate study for master's degree while training." Ten days after I submitted a resume to a box number, I was invited for an interview at the Brooklyn Public Library. I had little idea at that time about what librarians really did, and I envisioned the usual stereotypes. I'm ashamed to say that I prepared for the interview by taking off my makeup, pinning up my hair, and wearing my plainest dress. Fortunately, I was interviewed by a highly dedicated, enthusiastic, and skilled librarian who convinced me that librarianship presented a challenging, intellectually fascinating, and professionally rewarding career. I accepted the position as librarian trainee and quickly found out that she was right.

Subsequently I enrolled in the M.S. program at Columbia University's School of Library Service. Much of my time at the library was spent in the young teen department, where I started a book review newsletter for young people. After two years I left BPL to complete my master's program. My next position was as a school librarian in a New York City high school library. Again, I started a newsletter and a book club for students. Unfortunately, after the excitement of BPL, the bureaucracy of the Board of Education seemed stifling. I moved to the library of New York City Community College (now New York Technical College) the next year; again I edited a newsletter for faculty and students.

At NYCC I worked on acquisitions and collection development. We had twenty-six technical curricula to support and a generous budget. Unfortunately, the sources of materials for these curricula (e.g., fire science, tissue technology) were difficult to locate. So I began compiling a list of nontrade sources for technical-vocational curricula. At about that time I began participating in ALA and this provided the opportunity to meet the editors of several library publications. At their urging I wrote an article based upon my list about these sources for *Choice* and subsequently compiled a book for Bowker. I also wrote several articles about social responsibility and libraries for *Wilson Library Bulletin* and *Library Journal.*

My high level of professional involvement, and my writing and editing efforts, led to tenure and a promotion at NYCC, as well as an offer to join the staff of Bowker's *School Library Journal.* The opportunity to combine my library, writing, and publishing interests was too tempting to turn down, despite my tenured assistant professorship at the college. Having written a book for Bowker, I knew editors in the Book Division well and often suggested book ideas while working at *SLJ.* I was offered a position in the book division. During my tenure at Bowker I participated in numerous management and financial training opportunities offered by Bowker's then-parent company, Xerox Corporation. I also met Jack Neal, who was to become my partner. Though Jack and I learned a great deal about the business side of publishing, both of us gradually became frustrated with the bureaucracy and inflexibility of a large corporation. In 1976, we left Bowker to found Neal-Schuman Publishers, Inc.

NATURE OF THE WORK

My skills and education as a librarian have been invaluable to me in my present position as president of Neal-Schuman. Librarianship is, after all, a profession of searching and discovery. Librarians know how to find out *how* to find out. While I no longer decide what books to buy for a library collection, the success of our business depends on predicting what books librarians will buy. This is where my interest in and knowledge of the field, plus my contacts, are invaluable in obtaining manuscripts, identifying potential authors, and developing publication ideas.

As president of the firm I have the usual presidential duties and areas of responsibility, which I share with Jack. Together we publish, market, and sell books and journals. As in any business, we must maintain a reasonable financial basis, meet payrolls, and pay our bills, while keeping an eye on new developments in librarianship and the related information science disciplines.

Over the years we have hired a number of librarians to serve as editors and editorial assistants. Some of them have gone on to important posts in other areas of publishing. The library backgrounds of Neal-Schuman staff are important to the development of our publication list.

QUALIFICATIONS

My experience and education as a librarian, as well as my active participation in library associations, facilitates my work as a developer and publisher of works designed for library and information science professionals. Just knowing who would be able to suggest a likely writer of a particular book gives me the sort of access to prospective authors that is indispensable.

The ability to hire and supervise a staff is not something easily learned, but "the buck stops" with the owners of a small business. Recruiting and selecting the most promising applicant is not always easy. After that, keeping track of progress, motivating staff, and ensuring that they learn and grow is essential.

Having a partner removes much of the "lone wolf"

aspect entrepreneurs often experience, but choosing the *right* partner in any small business venture is critical. We have different, complementary backgrounds. Since I entered publishing at a fairly high editorial level, I lacked basic copyediting and production knowledge. Jack's solid editorial experience at Bowker involved essential skills needed for a successful publishing operation, while I brought the subject knowledge, contacts, and authors to the company. In addition, Jack was an experienced editor and compiler of large reference works, an excellent complement to my experience with journal articles, monographs, and smaller reference materials.

PROS AND CONS

Running a small business means you are always thinking about business projects and problems. Even on vacations I find myself wondering how things are going back at the office and often calling to find out. An entrepreneur never has a nine-to-five day or a two-day weekend.

My professional involvement, though certainly valuable to the business, has meant many midnight hours and lost weekends. Work at Neal-Schuman does not stop just because there's a speech to give in Oregon or a conference to attend in North Carolina.

There is no such thing as tenure for an entrepreneur. Nor is there any larger organization to provide cushioning from the ups and downs of the economy. In fact, the support system most of us are used to in work situations is simply not there. If you want the office cleaned or the trash taken out, you must make the arrangements to see that it is done.

Stamina, a sense of humor, and the belief that you can and will survive crises is essential for the small-business owner. Like a roller coaster, there are ups and downs.

Nevertheless, I would not want things any other way. My work is always interesting. There is great flexibility and no bureaucracy to second guess or slow down our work. Neal-Schuman has provided me with opportunities to travel, participate, meet many new and interesting people, and contribute something to the profession and our greater society. As ALA president I was able to initiate a major national public awareness campaign, "Call for America's Libraries: Say Yes to Your Right to Know," to bring attention to the funding crisis libraries now face.

Throughout my career I have sought out challenges and been willing to take risks. There are certainly days when I miss the security of working for a large organization, but I have never seriously regretted my decision.

Running a business is not for everyone, but as far as I'm concerned, this is the best job in the world!

MATTHEW J. VELLUCCI
FOUNDER AND PRESIDENT OF A FIRM PROVIDING CONTRACT STUDIES AND OPERATIONS FOR LIBRARIES

Matthew J. Vellucci is founder and president, Special Information Services, Inc., 7212 13th Ave., Takoma Park, MD 20912. He served in public, academic, and corporate libraries before becoming special assistant to the Dean at the College of Library and Information Services at the University of Maryland (1968-1970). He was employed by Herner & Company from 1970 to 1974, then in 1975 he established his own consulting business. He has been active in several trade and professional associations as well as research organizations. He was coauthor of a book on information systems and served as co-editor (first edition) of *The National Directory of State Government Agencies*.

INTRODUCTION

If it's a long way to Tipperary, it's a very long way from library school to library consulting. When I graduated from Columbia University thirty years ago I had not even heard of consulting in terms of libraries (and most others in our field hadn't either). But now, after seventeen years of independent consulting, the idea and practice are firmly entrenched.

The most immediate turn of events for me started in 1970, when I was hired as a senior analyst and librarian for Herner & Company, one of the oldest library and information science consulting firms in the country. This was to be my introduction to the consulting field. For the next four and a half years I not only managed the company library, but I also learned about the work entailed in providing consulting services on library or other information-related projects. I was involved in a nationwide study on library statistics for the National Center for Education Statistics, as well as other special studies for both government and private clients.

This apprenticeship, plus all my previous experience (with a public library system, college library, petroleum library, and as special assistant to the dean of a library school), served me well when I decided to take my chances and strike out on my own at the start of 1975. I was cautiously confident, but also aware that I was going into somewhat unexplored territory alone.

NATURE OF THE WORK

I consciously set out to establish a reputation as a small-business entrepreneur, not to build a large firm. Basically, I did not want to be bothered with all of the personnel and other administrative concerns that come with having a number of employees.

The work area I initially selected was that of special studies and surveys. In this concentration, I could draw upon my experience with Herner & Company, as well as be able to work independently and not worry about building an organization to handle projects. Soon after venturing out, I obtained my first work, a subcontract with Herner for a collection development study for one of the Navy libraries.

For eight or nine years my work was concentrated on special studies and surveys. These involved identifying problems and assessing situations, conducting user surveys, developing long- and short-range plans, and recommending improvements for libraries. Other specialized work included serving as an expert consultant on a report inventory project for a government agency, and preparing special reports and handbooks.

By chance, my work expanded into another area in the mid-1980s, one that I had not considered earlier. Since 1984, I have had contracts with two trade associations and one health-related research organization to manage and conduct their library operations. Because my firm is small (two full-time employees, including me), these contracts have involved work in small-scale facilities. The projects evolved initially from special study work first performed for the clients, who subsequently wanted to have continuing expertise available to help implement and manage operations, and who for various reasons did not want to go the route of having regular library employees. I have consciously not entered the information brokerage field as such. Many librarians are now engaged in this work, but I prefer to continue with those areas in which I have concentrated for so long.

Several opportunities have been afforded me by the work described above. One is being able to provide an organization with a fresh outlook or perspective on a matter and establish credibility in the process. As an outsider, I have no vested interest in promoting a certain approach or pursuing a certain direction. I just have the consultant's experienced view of what might be most appropriate in the circumstances. Not only can you help improve existing operations, but you can also be creative in helping to suggest and initiate new things or methods.

Because of the nature of my particular work, I have also had the opportunity to become acquainted with a variety of organizations, large and small, private and government, that cover a wide range of concerns, from banking, aluminum, and liquor, to cancer and workplace health. This has given me an invaluable perspective on how different organizations operate and how to approach their information situation and needs.

Another perspective is also provided by the opportunity not only to appraise existing facilities, but also to become involved in establishing a new library or information center. The work and problems dealing with an ongoing concern are quite different from those involving in new entity.

QUALIFICATIONS

For the type of work described above, probably the most important qualification is having broad-based working experience. This involves a knowledge of and familiarity with all types of library operations, including public and technical service activities. I also consider it valuable to have worked for other people for a number of years prior to going independent. Observing and learning how others approach various matters, helped me to develop a personal perspective on directions to take.

Some behavioral characteristics are also important for this kind of work. Specifically, you need vision, flexibility, and patience. You should be able to sift or sort out major matters or problems from minor ones, and establish priorities for working on them. You also need to be realistic in your approach to things. It is important to get the "feel" of an organization, so that your recommendations or steps you take are received positively. I have found it useful to suggest incremental rather than all-encompassing changes over a period of time. Most of the organizations I have dealt with are concerned with bottom-line output and economies of scale; they are more comfortable with step-by-step changes that do not inflate the budget unreasonably.

Sounding out an organization also helps you to know when might be the right time to suggest or implement changes. All of your ideas might appear feasible and appropriate, but if they do not coincide with an organization's plans or timetable for change, they might just as well be left unsaid. Knowing when to "strike" is as important as developing your plans for change.

Another useful qualification is being able to see how other resources within the organization might dovetail with library needs and activities. Positive, proactive cooperation with other units is essential. Contrary to what many librarians think today, I feel that it is not necessary for the library to try to do everything. Rather, it is more important that the library be outstanding in what it has selected to do. In this way a person's reputation and image are built.

Final ingredients for contract work are a network of personal contacts and good job performance; the latter leads to subsequent good references and a favorable reputation. In this line of work, it is also true that whom you know helps. At the same time, however, you must perform capably and responsibly if you hope to establish a reputation.

PROS AND CONS

What are the rewards of contract work? Along with probably every other library consultant, I would first mention the personal satisfaction of being independent. Not being tied to a regular schedule affords a flexibility that does wonders for the mind and body. This freedom also has some other benefits.

With no restrictions to a particular type of work or organization, you can be creative (within limits, of course), and can probably accomplish some things more easily than an employee could. You are more readily able to try new things or do things differently. Also, it is very much a learning experience; although the main problems or concerns are often the same, each organization is unique. How you handle this uniqueness is a clue to how successful you will be. There is a great personal satisfaction in jobs well done and seeing your reputation (as well as the library's) grow as a result of the confidence placed in you by others.

At the same time there are some serious disadvantages to contract consulting. First, because you are relying on yourself for income, you always have to be on the alert for new or continuing work. A successful reputation is no guarantee of future work (the recessions of 1981-82 and 1991-92 affected me as well as millions of others in the country). Although I have been fortunate most of my work has come via client references or other contacts, rather than active marketing, I still have to be concerned about the future.

Consulting work is also hectic most of the time. Juggling several contracts at the same time, splitting your attention among different concerns and activities of different clients, keeps you moving. Add to this the time required to write new proposals, discuss projected work with prospective clients, and attend to the regular administrative matters that are required in running a company, and you are left with little "free" time. You learn to relish the few times when the pace slows somewhat.

Consultants also have to expend energy on working with some clients who can be frustrating. I am lucky to have encountered only a few of these types in my years of working. But they are out there: organizations and people who cannot see the bigger picture or how things might best be accomplished. It is disheartening also when some projects turn out to be more in the nature of exercises than serious attempts at change. You may do your best, expending time and energy, but the client does nothing after accepting your report or plan. This applies also to those instances when proposals are submitted to prospective clients, and not a word of acknowledgement is received. It's all the more frustrating when you have been asked to do a proposal or some other preliminary work on a rush basis.

In summary, a consultant's career can be exhilarating, creative, satisfying. It can also be discouraging, frantic, and unstable. It certainly is not for everyone. Over the years several people have told me that they at times have considered going on their own, but the uncertainty of the situation, especially if one has a family to consider, was prohibitive for them. If, however, you can bring good working experience as a librarian, managerial qualities, and good personal characteristics to the job, it is an alternative career worth considering. But make sure you have lined up that first contract being going out on your own.

EMPLOYEES

TONI CARBO BEARMAN
(WITH SUSAN WEBRECK ALMAN)
PROFESSIONAL EDUCATORS IN LIBRARY AND
INFORMATION SCIENCES

Toni Carbo Bearman is dean and professor at the School of Library and Information Science, University of Pittsburgh, 505 Lis Building, 135 N. Bellefield Ave., Pittsburgh, PA 15260. After working in several libraries, she served as executive director of the National Federation of Abstracting and Indexing Services (NFAIS). From 1980 to 1986 she was executive director of the U.S. National Commission on Libraries and Information Science (NCLIS); she then moved to her present position. She has an A.B. from Brown University and an M.S. and a Ph.D. from Drexel University, from which she also received a Distinguished Alumni Award. Ms. Bearman has been active in many organizations, including the American Society for Information Science (serving as its president during 1990—1991), the Special Libraries Association, the International Federation for Information and Documentation (serving as chair of several FID committees), the National Information Standards Organization (NISO), and other organizations for information professionals. She has also received awards from several of these groups. She has published more than 80 articles and is coeditor of *The International Information and Library Review*.

INTRODUCTION

My entry into the realm of education began nearly thirty years ago when I joined the American Mathematical Society as a bibliographic assistant in the library. Since that time I have enjoyed each of my positions, ranging from an engineering library subject specialist to executive director of the U.S. National Commission on Libraries and Information Science. These years of opportunity within the profession, coupled with research and writing interests, led me to my current position in higher education.

I have long had definite views about the importance of high standards in schools preparing information professionals; these viewpoints have been strengthened through my experience as an educator and my participation in professional activities. I am especially aware of the need for faculty with a strong commitment to teaching, research, and community service. These three qualities are inherently necessary in order to educate individuals to take a leading role in an information-intensive society and to impart a sense of professionalism. Students profit from having faculty with diverse backgrounds, differing points of view, and practical experience. The community of special librarians has these qualifications, and many special librarians may be interested in a career as a professional educator.

NATURE OF THE WORK

Faculty in colleges and universities devote most of their time to three primary academic responsibilities: teaching, research and communicating the results of research, and community service. Each of these three areas involves different knowledge and skills, and each overlaps with the others. Time devoted to the three varies considerably among schools and individuals.

Teaching requires much more than lecturing in front of a class. Effective teaching requires extensive knowledge of the information field and in-depth knowledge of at least one specialty. This knowledge must be kept current through reading the literature, research, participating in professional associations, networking with other experts, getting hands-on experience, and other continuing education activities. In order to be an effective teacher, faculty must be able to develop a course syllabus that is relevant to the needs and interests of the students and that defines and meets clear educational objectives. Good teaching also requires good organization and communication skills. Selecting course materials for the students' use requires knowledge of the current literature, effective use of audiovisual materials, the integration of hands-on experience using technologies into the course, and, increasingly, the use of multimedia instruction tools. Full participation in the school's curriculum development is another critical component of teaching.

In addition to regular courses within the program, many schools provide continuing education programs, and faculty may teach special courses, workshops, or institutes, perhaps during weekends or evenings or over the summer, often for additional pay. These teaching activities are essential to effective education of the students.

In addition, faculty must be available to meet with students to discuss course assignments, to assist them with program and career goals, to evaluate students during comprehensive examinations, and to advise them on graduate research projects and oversee theses and dissertations. Other teaching activities include serving on a variety of committees related to education within the department, school, and university. These committee assignments may range from curriculum or strategic planning to athletics.

Research is another essential component of a faculty's responsibilities, and there are many valid reasons for conducting it. It is critical for faculty members to conduct research that adds to the existing body of knowledge. Both theoretical and applied research are essential to the growth of the discipline upon which the profession is based. Research results are communicated by faculty in scholarly and professional publications. These publications are vehicles for new information or theories to be shared with professional colleagues. They are also essential to the tenure process since the vast majority of faculty positions are in the tenure stream.

The tenure process varies from institution to institution,

but it almost always involves meeting standards of high-quality work and promise of continued contributions. A faculty member's record is reviewed by his or her peers after several (usually six) years and evaluated for evidence of excellence in teaching, research and communication of research results, and community service.

Involvement in professional activities, commonly referred to as community service, is of special concern to faculty in a professional school. Contributions to the profession and to the broader society are considered to be fundamental responsibilities of a faculty member. Faculty are expected to be involved in their profession, as active members in professional organizations, consultants, speakers at conferences, and project participants. Also, their involvement with professional associations is an excellent means of interacting with professionals, keeping current on trends and activities, and working to promote the profession.

QUALIFICATIONS

Successful educators must have good oral and written communication skills. In addition, they must possess detailed knowledge of some special fields as well as awareness of the varied information sources touching on these subjects. Enthusiasm about the subject being taught and teaching are also very important. Educators must enjoy teaching and working with students.

Besides being skilled at lecturing and planning courses, they must continue to do independent research, hence the requirement that most regular, full-time faculty members usually have Ph.D. There are instances, of course, where special librarians have stepped into a faculty position without a doctoral degree, but the most likely candidate will have completed the Ph.D., especially for tenure-stream positions. Usually the degree is in the field of library and information science, but occasionally a doctorate in another discipline may be accepted. Requirements for faculty positions also include not only a demonstrated ability to teach and undertake research but also a record of publications and involvement in professional activities.

There are opportunities for special librarians to attain faculty positions in the information professions in several different ways. First, they might consider an adjunct appointment. Adjunct faculty who are not permanent faculty members usually receive appointments on a term-by-term basis. Often adjuncts have full-time positions within a library or information center, and because of their subject expertise, interest in working with students and time commitments, they teach a single course on a special topic (such as law librarianship or resources in business and industry).

Opportunities also exist for individuals who can teach continuing education workshops and institutes, often offered as noncredit programs—although some may be offered for credit. Many times special librarians have the expertise that is needed to provide programs for those who are continuing to update their professional skills. Usually, these continuing education activities are provided over concentrated periods of time, such as a one-week workshop or an institute over three weekends. Often, these programs are designed to be revenue-generating, or at least self-supporting, and require a minimum number of students.

PROS AND CONS

Being a faculty member has many rewards. The opportunity of working with students and assisting in the education of future colleagues is very satisfying. I find teaching to be stimulating; it forces my outlook to stay fresh. I always find that I learn at least as much from my students as I teach them. Listening to their questions, watching the excitement as they learn, and realizing that I may have contributed in some small way to their thinking and growing are invigorating and extremely rewarding experiences.

In addition, the opportunities provided for research and intellectual stimulation far surpass those of many other positions. Having the opportunity to explore ideas and theories and to test them in collaboration with other scholars is challenging and fulfilling. Hammering out drafts of articles and subjecting them to rigorous peer review, then revising them and repeating the process until an article or report is ready for publication is demanding but satisfying. Research and teaching also provide the opportunity to work in collaboration with others from different specialties and disciplines, often across institutional and even national boundaries. At some universities faculty receive support for travel to professional conferences; sometimes they are provided with workstations, computer laboratories, and networks and other technological resources, as well as student assistants for teaching, research, and other needs.

Within the academic environment, schedules for faculty are more flexible than those within other types of institutions, and this flexibility provides an excellent opportunity to work from home or other locations and to devote blocks of time to specific projects. In most universities, faculty are encouraged to devote up to one day a week to consulting to keep them current with the practice of our profession.

Being encouraged (and often supported) to participate in community service within the university and, in many schools, within the wider community of which the university is part, is another plus for careers in academia. Working on university-wide committees to improve the quality of student life or library services, participating actively in professional societies, or contributing as a volunteer to an adult literacy program or a neighborhood association are all rewarding activities. University communities are usually culturally rich and ethnically diverse, and provide a wonderfully interesting environment within which to live and raise a family.

There are a few negative aspects of being a faculty member. The most obvious one is that many colleges and universities pay less than corporations. Many also have less money to support travel, and provide hardware, software, and other resources. Of course, this varies considerably among institutions.

The investment in the Ph.D. necessary for most full-time, tenure-stream faculty positions is significant, both in dollars and time, and not everyone is interested in committing his or her time and money to the advanced degree. The academic rigor of courses, research, writing publications, and teaching is not to everyone's taste or interest. Also, academic institutions, while stimulating to some, may seem painfully slow and impractical. Sometimes a fine scholar put into a management position is not always a good manager, and this many be very frustrating to someone accustomed to trained managers. Decision making by consensus may also be annoying to those accustomed to more hierarchical structures. However, in my thirty years in the information field, I have never seen the "ivory tower" the stereotype suggests. Good colleges and universities are very practical and are in touch with the real world. All of the elements of industry, government, and many other institutions, such as management issues, fiscal realities, politics, accountability, and other "real-world" concerns are alive and well in academia.

The schedule flexibility may not be to everyone's liking. While a faculty member is not restricted by a specific schedule, the successful individual must be disciplined in order to complete work and be at the cutting edge; these pressures may seem excessive to some individuals. Expectations are high, and the pressures of teaching, working with students, conducting research, and publishing—while remaining active in the profession—may seem too demanding for those who would prefer a job with a fewer number of responsibilities. Also, some people find students' interests and demands difficult. Just as with many other careers, a faculty member is in a rigorous and demanding position that can be rewarding and frustrating, sometimes at the same time.

For those not put off by the nature of academic institutions, a career as a faculty member is extremely rewarding. It provides the opportunity to work with future colleagues and help them learn and grow. Academia also provides a structure for collaborative research and the communication of research results, with peer review and evaluation. A teaching career encourages you to keep abreast of the newest developments in the discipline, while remaining involved in the practice of your profession. The university community is a learning environment within a culturally diverse and exciting broader community. Special librarians should consider carefully the many opportunities provided by a career in professional education.

THOMAS CREAMER
LEXICOGRAPHER FOR A FOREIGN LANGUAGE DICTIONARY PUBLISHER

Thomas Creamer is employed as a lexicographer by MRM, Inc., P.O. Box 400, Kensington, MD 20895. A research firm, MRM publishes reference works and teaching materials for Asian and African languages. Mr Creamer has a B.A. from Bradley University, an M.A. from University of Virginia, and an M.L.S degree from the University of Maryland. He has compiled two Chinese language dictionaries and has been active in the Modern Language Association.

INTRODUCTION

For the last fifteen years I have been employed as a lexicographer by MRM, Inc., of Kensington, MD., a research firm in the Washington, D.C., area that is primarily devoted to publishing African and Asian language teaching materials and reference works. Over the years I have worked on a number of projects involving several languages, but my main activity has been the compilation of a large Chinese-English dictionary-database of approximately 220,000 entries. This specific project is sponsored by the CETA (Chinese-English Translation Assistance) Group, a cooperative effort involving government, academic, and private sponsors, and is managed by MRM. I first became aware of MRM through a colleague in the Special Collections section of the Alderman Library at

The opinions expressed in this article are those of the author and do not reflect those of MRM, Inc. or the CETA Group. The author would like to thank John E. Taube, Reference Librarian at Georgetown University, for commenting on drafts of this paper.

the University of Virginia, where I worked as a reference assistant while completing my master's degree in East Asian history. After graduation I worked on the CETA project for two years as a volunteer (I was employed at the College of William and Mary during this time as the director of an Asian studies residence hall) and was then hired first as a part-time employee, and later as a full-time linguist at MRM. My years as a volunteer proved instrumental not only in my being hired for the position, but also as a training period or apprenticeship where I was able to learn the craft (not necessarily art) of bilingual lexicography and, equally important, become familiar with the vast reference bibliography.

NATURE OF THE WORK

When you begin to delve into the intricacies of language you almost immediately become acutely aware of your limitations, linguistic and otherwise. The familiar soon seems strange and the unfamiliar becomes ever so mind-boggling. Faced with the proposition of writing dozens, if not hundreds, of definitions a day, the lexicographer must quickly and accurately digest the collected information (i.e., citations), reflect on his or her own understanding of the entry word, surreptitiously survey the competition (i.e., other dictionaries), and draft a "unique" and, it is hoped, brilliant definition. The difficulty of these matters is compounded considerably in bilingual lexicography, you must not only define the entry word but also interpret the cultural nuances of the word being defined, as well as the defining words. In dealing with a language such as Chinese, with its several thousand years of written records, not to mention its ideographic writing system, the task at hand can only be described as humbling. Without the proper resources, the task would be virtually impossible.

In essence, lexicography, monolingual or bilingual, is reference. Once the word list for the dictionary or glossary has been determined, one of the lexicographer's most important tasks is to assemble a library of reference materials. The materials include not only citational sources such as books, newspapers, and the like, but also related dictionaries and all matter of reference works, including concordances, maps, recordings, and technical manuals, to name but a few. The library I have built to support my work contains approximately several thousand items covering topics from agronomy to astronomy. Obviously, in a major publishing house a more extensive collection is necessary. For example, Houghton Mifflin Company, which publishes *The American Heritage Dictionary of the English Language*, has a reference library staffed by six librarians and features more than fifteen sources, supplemented by six hundred periodical subscriptions and access to numerous online databases. Whatever the size of the dictionary or the company producing it, the quality of the library is often reflected in the quality of the dictionary.

Dictionaries are compiled one entry at a time. The entry generally consist of four parts: the entry word, the pronunciation, rendering, labels, and the definition itself. Many entries also require careful cross-referencing, usage notes, and indication of variants. Each component of the entry demands equal treatment, with danger lurking at virtually every turn. For entry selection in Chinese, for example, you have to be alert to the differences among the languages used in the People's Republic of China (PRC), the Republic of China (ROC, i.e., Taiwan), and the Overseas Chinese communities (e.g., Singapore), not to mention dialectical uses within each area. The differences are not only in the style of Chinese character used (i.e, simplified characters in the PRC and complex characters elsewhere), but also the form characters used to write the entry.

Pronunciation, including four basic tones in Standard Chinese and as many as eight in certain dialects, can be given in a number of romanization systems or in any of several Chinese-character-derived schemes. Labels, especially for grammar, are usually the easiest part of the definition to deal with because they are generally omitted in Chinese sources. The first systematic treatment of Chinese grammar did not appear until the end of the nineteenth century, and much work remains to be done. Chinese sources will hint at part of speech by the way in which the entry word is defined, and it is not uncommon for the included citations to hint at a different part of speech. If the project requires grammar labels, their accurate and consistent rendering may well be the most difficult part of the entry to compile. In almost all other cases, writing the definition (in all of its meanings) will be the crux of the matter.

The definitions must be approached within the scope of the dictionary, but with Chinese you can easily become distracted by the richness of the language and the need to constantly interpret cultural nuances. For example, the saying that translates as "mend the fold after losing the sheep" means exactly the opposite in Chinese from what it does in English (i.e., it's not too late for action). This is one of the thousands of "false friends" in the two languages, where what seems familiar is anything but friendly. Compared to entries of this kind, defining terms from the latest scientific breakthroughs or recent policy pronouncements from the PRC government can seem almost routine.

In coping with all of these matters, the lexicographer is not unlike the reference librarian. It is not the job of the lexicographer to know the reliability of each word, its pronunciation, definition, or whatever from memory, just as it is not the job of the reference librarian to know the answers to the questions posed every day at the reference desk. It is the job of both, however, to find the answer, and find it quickly. Finding the meaning of the "image of the two clocks" as used by Leibniz or where St. Alfonso, the beheaded one, accomplished his conversions is akin to defining Mao Zedong's phrase "one divides into two" or the "Tian'anmen Massacre." The references sources are the key to the puzzle. If the lexicographer had to rely on his or her own knowledge to compile a dictionary, the resulting work for most of us mortals would most likely be a pocket dictionary. Similarly, if a reference librarian were without the reference collection, the line at the reference desk would be short indeed.

Maintenance of the reference collection then is of vital importance to the lexicographer. In a small operation, which most dictionary-making concerns are, the lexicographer often oversees the library. In this respect the lexicographer is purely, and not so simply, a librarian and needs to hone librarian skills. Sources must be identified, located, evaluated, purchased, cataloged, and shelved. The task is somewhat more difficult and frustrating when dealing with Chinese sources because they often take months to locate and acquire. Planned buying is virtually impossible and blanket orders are too expensive. In any case, the librarian/lexicographer needs to be constantly on the lookout for potentially useful sources. One of my main activities during trips to China is to purchase books. Fortunately, Chinese books are one of the last bargains in China, so you can acquire many sources for a relatively small amount of money. Shipping the books home and eventually receiving them is another matter entirely, as I have lost scores of books in the mail. The maddening aspect of losing books is not necessarily the monetary loss, but the difficulty in finding the books again because of the crude book distribution system in China, where it is virtually impossible to find the book again or order it unless you have some connections with the publisher. Luckily, I have colleagues in the dictionary and publishing business who send me sources they think might be useful, and I do the same for them. It is not uncommon for me to carefully evaluate a source after, not before, it is purchased. Chinese bookstores are always crowded and it is difficult at best to go through the steps necessary to determine the precise value of the book. It is often easier to buy a book that costs the equivalent of one U.S. dollar and ship it home for evaluation than try to determine on the spot its applicability to the project. Just as in any library, shelving is important. I recently found a chemistry dictionary that I thought had been lost. The dictionary was shelved (most likely by me and before I went to library school) with some seldom-used general language materials, and I was able to find it only while desperately looking for something else. Without a doubt there have been dozens of occasions since the move where that dictionary would have been helpful. With the well-maintained library in place, the librarian/lexicographer becomes the lexicographer/reference librarian as he or she goes about the work using the appropriate sources.

QUALIFICATIONS

From the discussion above it should not be surprising that some of the qualifications for a reference librarian are the same for a (bilingual) lexicographer. Anyone looking at recent job announcements no doubt has seen ads that require at least one postgraduate degree, knowledge of a foreign language, computer fluency, and several years of experience, not to mention dynamism and a pleasant disposition. These are also the basic qualifications for a lexicographer. An advanced degree in linguistics or related discipline is often required. Obviously for the bilingual lexicographer, training in a foreign language is a sine qua non. Within these areas there are many diverse paths that can lead to lexicography. In my own case, for example, my academic training was in Chinese history, not languages per se. I read a great deal of Chinese material for the degree, which proved a good substitute for in-depth linguistic studies, supplemented by my undergraduate and graduate courses in Chinese language.

Besides academic training, the most important qualification for the job is attention to detail. Each entry in each of its parts rivets the attention, and no part can be neglected or shortchanged. Almost equally important is the ability to make a decision. You have to define the entry in some manner and often you do not have the time or resources to consult colleagues in the field. You can sometimes "weasel" a definition by saying it "is something like..." or it is "a kind of...," but a decision must be made, and it had better be the right one. Another qualification is what is sometimes called in the profession "an iron buttocks," which is the ability to sit alone at your desk for long periods of time and focus on the work at hand. Finally, you need to continue refining and updating your knowledge and skills. Languages change and so must the lexicographer. By reading outside the job, conferring with colleagues at professional meetings, and traveling, the lexicographer needs to keep learning, and inquiring.

PROS AND CONS

The primary reward of lexicography comes from the work itself. Samuel Johnson's infamous characterization of the lexicographer as "a harmless drudge" is only slightly amusing to most lexicographers. The work is neither. Lexicographers working in a totalitarian country knows full well that the authorities do not look on their work as "harmless." Anyone misinformed by an incorrect definition also knows the kind of harm a lexicographer can cause. As for "drudgery," if learning new things continually and having your intellect challenged every day on the job is "drudgery," then so be it.

In addition to the work, there are also opportunities to meet with colleagues in interesting places. The two major lexicographic organizations, the Dictionary Society of North American and the European Association for Lexicography, hold conferences every two years in locations ranging from Columbia, Missouri, to Cleveland, Ohio, to Zurich, Switzerland, to Malaga, Spain. There is also a Lexicography Discussion Group, part of the Modern Language Association, which meets annually. The Conferences offer the opportunity to commiserate with fellow "drudges" and, not insignificant, get out of the office.

On the negative side, there is indeed a certain drudgery to the work. There are days when the last thing you can stomach is to have yet another entry appear on the screen or on a card in front of your face. With large dictionary projects there can also be the frustration of working on a dictionary for years before it is finally in print for the world (and especially your family) to see. Even then it is sometimes hard to be able to point at exactly what is was that you did to make it a success.

The biggest drawback to the profession is the small number of jobs in the field. The major publishing houses employ only a few full-time lexicographers, opting instead for consultants and part-time workers. For example, the preface to the revised edition of the *Random House Dictionary of the English Language,* perhaps the largest English-language dictionary project in the United States since the publication of *Webster's Third New International Dictionary*, lists only thirty-seven editors and editorial assistants (i.e., lexicographers). Even after you find a job, however, it will often be only short-term. Many lexicographers are hired only for a specific project, and are terminated once that project is completed.

Besides commercial publishing houses, there are a number of lexicographic projects in the academic world where a librarian with some knowledge of lexicography may apply his or her skills. At the University of Georgia, for instance, there is a project in its initial stages to compile a *Dictionary of Briticisms*, and the University of Wisconsin is in the final stages of publishing the much heralded *Dictionary of American Regional English*. Similarly, there may be opportunities for the librarian/ lexicographer/archivist working with special dictionary collections, such as the Cordell Collection of Rare and Early Dictionaries at Indiana State University; with publishing house records such as the Merriam-Webster collection at Beinecke Library of Yale

University; or with the papers of important lexicographers
and dictionary enthusiasts, such as the Peter Tamony files at
the University of Missouri-Columbia.

When compared to lexicography, there is an abundance
of jobs for librarians. Be that as it may, those interested in
pursuing this career path may be interested in special training
in lexicography. Indiana State University, the University of
Pennsylvania, and Southern Illinois University have from time
to time offered courses in lexicography. In Europe, the
Dictionary Research Centre at the University of Exeter, the
URA SILEX at the University of Lille III, and the Vakgroep
Lexicologie of the Vrije Universiteit Amsterdam offer
diploma courses at the graduate level in lexicography. With
some training, imagination, and good luck you should be able
to use the skills common to lexicography and librarianship to
enhance your employment opportunities.

ANN MARIE CUNNINGHAM
EXECUTIVE DIRECTOR OF A NONPROFIT MEMBERSHIP ORGANIZATION FOR INFORMATION PRODUCERS AND DISTRIBUTORS

Ann Marie Cunningham is executive director of the National Federation of Abstracting and Information Services (NFAIS), 1429 Walnut St., Philadelphia, PA 19102. After several years as periodicals librarian at a university library, she became an educational lecturer for the Institute for Scientific Information, followed by serving for several years as head of the Product Planning and Promotion Department at BIOSIS. In 1991 she was appointed to her present position at NFAIS. She has a B.A. from Notre Dame College of Staten Island (St. John's University) and an M.L.S. from Villanova University.

INTRODUCTION

The road to becoming executive director of an internationally recognized, nonprofit membership organization for producers, distributors, and users of information has been an exciting and challenging one. My love for books, libraries, and information dates as far back as I can remember. In grammar school and high school, when my classmates were signing up for sports teams or drama club, I joined the library club. Membership in the library club afforded me the opportunity to preview the new library materials before they went into general circulation.

NFAIS is a registered trademark of the National Federation of Abstracting and Information Services

As an English major in college, I usually could be found in my special corner of the college library reading vast amounts of the world's literature. What a wonderful racket, I thought, to earn a degree for doing what I loved best! Upon graduation from college, I served as a social worker in Spanish Harlem for a year. When I realized that this was not the career for me, I returned to my first love—libraries.

I entered the graduate library school program at Villanova University and was fortunate enough to land a job in the periodicals section of the university library. This enabled me to combine theoretical classroom knowledge with practical experience. Since the Periodicals Department contained the abstracting and indexing services, I had plenty of experience with these reference tools.

When I received my library degree, the director offered me the position of head of the Periodicals Department. I became the first Villanova University librarian to receive training on the use of online information services. During the next eight years, I conducted formalized training on the use of abstracting and indexing services, in addition to maintaining the periodicals collection.

After ten years at Villanova, I was ready for some new challenges. A former Villanova University circulation librarian who had gone to work for the Institute for Scientific Information (ISI) suggested that I apply for an open educational lecturer's position at ISI. He had found the private sector to be challenging and rewarding and thought that I would also.

ISI required that its educational lecturers have experience as professional librarians. It would be easier for a librarian to relate to the needs of the audience since so many audiences consisted of librarians, faculty, and students. Previous reference experience also enabled the Educational Lecturer to understand how ISI's products compared with those of the competition.

ISI's educational lecturers trained on the concept of citation indexing, the use of the print indexes, the online files, and, later, the database management software that ISI had begun to sell. While educational lecturers always had been part of the marketing staff, ISI had made a careful and deliberate delineation between training and sales positions. Educational Lecturers *supported* the sales staff's efforts.

Over time, educational lecturers began to play a larger role in the product development function, testing new products and services. Once the product was deemed ready to be launched, it usually was the educational lecturer who would introduce it at an exhibit, product review, or new training session.

While at ISI, I was encouraged to participate in the National Federation of Abstracting and Information Services (NFAIS) as a member of the Education Committee. ISI was one of the first for-profit members of NFAIS. The Education Committee afforded me the opportunity to share tips and "war stories" with trainers in other NFAIS member companies. NFAIS had begun publishing the *NFAIS Trainer's Circuit*, and I became its first editor. The newsletter contained practical information on meeting locations, training room setup, travel tips, and audiovisual material design for trainers within information companies.

After four and a half years at ISI, I was recruited by the director of marketing at BIOSIS for the position of section chief of product development. In addition to developing new product concepts to extend the BIOSIS product line, my staff and I conducted competitive analyses and feasibility studies. After one year, my duties were expanded to include the marketing function. As head of the newly-created Product Planning and Promotion Department, I was now responsible for advertising, direct mail, and sales tracking, in addition to product development.

Since my work at BIOSIS did not involve training, I gave up my participation in the NFAIS Education Committee and joined the NFAIS Publications Committee instead. Eventually, I became chairperson of this committee.

In 1991, the executive director's position at NFAIS became available. The previous director encouraged me to apply for the position on the strength of my professional experience and my long (twelve-year) association with and active participation in NFAIS. I became executive director of NFAIS in March 1991.

NATURE OF THE WORK

The National Federation of Abstracting and Information Services was founded in 1958. It is a membership organization comprising more than sixty five leading information producers, distributors, and users. NFAIS dedicates itself to the enhancement and advancement of the information industry by:

- facilitating the exchange of information among NFAIS members;

- presenting the collective opinion of NFAIS members to the industry;

- sponsoring timely and topical conferences;

- offering courses and informative members-only meetings;

- publishing newsletters, books, reports, and codes of practice; and

- encouraging cooperation among secondary information services.

NFAIS functions as a coordinating body for its member organizations. Member organizations contribute to NFAIS courses, conferences, publications, and research projects by encouraging their professional staff to serve on the NFAIS board of directors, any of the five NFAIS Working Committees (Common Practices and Standards, Education, Information Policy and Copyright, Membership, and Publications), or the *NFAIS Newsletter* Editorial Advisory Board.

As executive director, I am the senior executive of the Federation and report to the board of directors. I am responsible for implementation of all board policies and directives and for ensuring that NFAIS business is conducted according to the bylaws of the federation.

Some of my primary duties include:

- making arrangements for board and general assembly meetings;

- making arrangements and working with the program organizers for the annual conference;

- coordinating committee activities and serving as an ex-officio member of all committees;

- managing headquarters staff, including hiring, supervision, and performance evaluation of personnel;

- providing fiscal management for NFAIS, including preparing financial reports, preparing draft budgets for the board, and overseeing the receipt and disbursement of all funds;

- working with the Education Committee to oversee development of new training courses that are current and topical;

- working with the Membership Committee to recruit new members and retain current members;

- overseeing all NFAIS publications, including editing the *NFAIS Newsletter*, and writing and editing other publications, as appropriate;

- making presentations about NFAIS at library schools and public meetings;

- representing NFAIS in its interactions with other professional organizations, such as the Association of Information and Dissemination Centers (ASIDIC), the Coalition for Networked Information, the Information Industry Association, and the Special Libraries Association;

- working with the standards community to develop and review standards; and

- coordinating government relations activities, including keeping abreast of developments of interest to NFAIS members and ensuring NFAIS participation in pertinent activities.

QUALIFICATIONS

The basic educational requirement for becoming executive director of NFAIS is a B.A. or B.S.A. higher degree is preferred. In my opinion, an M.L.S. and/or M.B.A. is particularly useful for the foundation each provides in information dissemination and business practice. An understanding of the role that secondary information services play in information distribution is essential. Knowledge of the information industry is helpful.

Other qualifications include a minimum of five years administrative and management experience. Prior experience in membership development is useful, but not essential.

On a daily basis, the executive director interacts with a numerous of people with different levels of understanding of the information industry. The director must be able to communicate effectively both orally and in writing to advance the goals of NFAIS.

PROS AND CONS

As executive director of an internationally recognized information organization, I gain a bird's-eye view of the information industry. It is necessary to keep track of all of the influences (technological, economic, social, political, etc.) that come to bear on the industry and keep the membership informed of their potential impact. This responsibility is a tall order and both a pro and a con, since it requires constant review of the professional and trade literature and press releases, as well as personal networking.

The position offers a wide range of activity from conference and meeting planning, to writing and editing, to administrative duties. The position also offers high visibility through publications, presentations, and representation of NFAIS in dealings with other professional organizations.

On the negative side, it seems as if there is never enough time to accomplish all that must be done. Because the board and committee members are all volunteers, it sometimes takes longer to accomplish certain tasks than originally scheduled.

In general, however, I find the position of executive director of NFAIS to be both professionally and personally rewarding. Professional networking often leads to the development of lasting personal friendships.

I would encourage any librarian seeking a career change from a traditional library position to consider a career in a professional or trade organization. The variety of such organizations is as diverse as the range of special library positions.

LLOYD DAVIDSON
DEVELOPER OF EXPERT SYSTEMS, HYPERTEXT AND MULTIMEDIA SOFTWARE AT A UNIVERSITY

Lloyd Davidson is life sciences librarian and head, Access Services, Seeley G. Mudd Library for Science and Engineering, Northwestern University, Evanston, IL 60208. Following employment as a biology professor and director of the Electron Microscopy Laboratory at the University of Notre Dame, he moved to Northwestern University, where he serves as assistant director of the Seeley G. Mudd Library for Science and Engineering. He has a B.A. and an M.A. in paleontology and a Ph.D. in cell biology and zoology from the University of California, Berkeley, as well as an M.L.S. from Indiana University.

INTRODUCTION

Developing expert systems and hypertext multimedia programs is becoming an increasingly important part of all instructional endeavors, including those in libraries. Skill in the manipulation of such materials, and their artful incorporation into the workplace, provides a means of efficiently transferring information throughout our profession and will ensure that we adequately address today's technological changes in information management. Failure to learn to work with these technologies will likely result in our profession becoming one in which such programs are developed primarily by outside entrepreneurs, a group over whom we have no control, with results that could be disastrous to the integrity, self-sufficiency, and, ultimately, to the very existence of our profession.

Expert systems are not in danger of replacing librarians

or any other professionals, at least not at their current level of sophistication, but they can significantly augment our abilities and knowledge. This potential ensures that they will occupy a secure and expanding niche in all academic professions.

NATURE OF THE WORK

Expert system development is only one of several computer programming projects in which I am currently involved, all of which are, in a sense, extracurricular. My early work on expert systems for reference led to a beneficial faculty association. That in turn led to two other major projects—a multimedia NOTIS staff training program developed with KnowledgePro which contains graphics, hypertext, and expert systems components, and an Apple Library of Tomorrow (ALOT) grant to develop a standardized front end to various NOTIS Online Public Access Catalogs (OPACs) and other online bibliographic databases.

Besides work on reference-related expert system programs, I have developed hypertext programs for reference assistance and have worked on the design of Smart Forms for Inter-Library Loan. Smart Forms (forms that adjust their questions depending on the user responses) are destined to find application in nearly every department in the library, from ordering and acquisition to personnel and preservation.

This work with expert systems, Smart Forms, hypertext programs, and other multimedia applications involves grant writing, programming, systems analysis, and administration. While such program development is only one of my duties, and in fact is not even part of my official job description, it does occupy a very significant proportion of my time. Unfortunately, because these duties are not part of my official job description, this work is done in addition to my other duties rather than representing a true alternative career.

Administration of these projects includes finding

support money and capable development staff. Like most academic institutions, Northwestern University has the benefit of a very capable pool of undergraduates who appreciate working on interesting projects. These students, with financial support from the federal work-study program, have provided several very fine programmers at relatively low cost.

One of the reasons I believe I have had such good success in finding dedicated undergraduate programmers to help in these projects is that I give them their share of credit in papers and talks and because I give them as much freedom and latitude as possible in designing the program. This has provided them with a feeling of creative involvement in its outcome and has made them feel more than simply employees.

Developing collaborative associations with faculty and computer center programmers has also been of critical importance to the success of these endeavors. Besides providing essential expert guidance, and access to exceptionally talented graduate students, such contacts have furnished coinvestigators for research grant applications that, in turn, have supplied part of the funds and equipment needed to support such projects. Since practicing librarians do not normally have graduate students, even when they have faculty status (which I do not), it is important for us to develop cooperative faculty contacts and, in my case at least, the Council on Library Resources Collaborative Faculty/Librarian Research Grants have been instrumental in helping to form such connections. Being able to provide even a small amount of research funding is a great help in building peer-based professional relationships with research faculty.

Expert system, hypertext, and multimedia program development is largely unexplored territory and involves efforts in specialties such as the design of human-computer interfaces and educational technology, subjects in which I have no training. This has required many hours of outside reading, intensive program evaluation and testing, and discussion with others before I have obtained products with which I am even partially satisfied. In general such projects require extensive work beyond the standard work week, work for which the only credit I can reasonably expect is personal satisfaction, certainly not remunerative rewards or often even immediate peer recognition.

QUALIFICATIONS

Interest is the primary qualification needed, as well as sufficient time to commit to such time-consuming projects. Interest grows with the project, and the time must be extracted from other parts of your life. I firmly believe that interest in any field is an acquired taste that develops along with knowledge of and activity in a field. My own professional training until 1982 was in cell biology, and only since my entry into the library profession have I gained any significant knowledge of computers and programming. Along with this knowledge, my interest in information and library science disciplines, and my appreciation of their intellectual content, has grown as well, not replacing but certainly now on a par with my love of biology.

There was a time when expert system programming was a very daunting undertaking which required highly developed programming skills in arcane languages. This is no longer the case. With the development of expert system shells, programs that incorporate easy to manipulate if-then logic rules and basic formatting, and easier to use programming languages like Visual Basic and QuickBasic, such program development has become accessible even to those with limited computer backgrounds. An example of this appeared in a recent article in the *Chronicle of Higher Education* on how the NeXT computer has simplified educational program development at Allegheny College. (1)

In the specific expert system area in which I have

worked, developing science reference support programs, a knowledge of science has certainly been helpful, but domain expertise is not essential since you can always call upon experts for support in those fields in which your personal knowledge is limited.

In any project involving software development a working knowledge of the fundamentals of the computer systems being used is certainly necessary, including some basic hardware familiarity. But, as I said earlier, the programs are becoming simple enough that extensive knowledge is no longer essential for success.

PROS AND CONS

One of the most attractive aspects of any programming job is the feeling of completion when a program actually performs as you intended it to. If the program turns out to be of real benefit to you or others in the workplace, your satisfaction is that much greater. In the case of expert system and multimedia development you have the additional incentive of knowing that you are helping to develop an area which is likely to have very significant impact on the profession over the next several years.

Work on these programs has also led to a number of speaking engagements, to papers on the topic (including this one), and, along with several other colleagues (Judy Myers, University of Houston, Craig Robertson; University of Vermont; Roy Chang, Northeastern Illinois University; and John Richardson, University of California, Los Angeles), to participation in a series of expert system workshops for LITA, ASIS, and other associations.

One of the drawbacks of working in this area is the lack of widespread support for or understanding of such development by library administrators and the difficulty, in my case, of working largely as a committee of one within the library. This sense of isolation has been partially alleviated by the collaborative support I have found from faculty outside the library. Such isolation is not the case in every institution, of course. At the University of Houston, for example, Judy Myers has worked for several years with a team of coworkers to develop the Reference Expert program, yet even there funding has been very limited, development software is difficult to finance, and staff must divide their time between software development and other duties. Time is one of the most important commodities in such project development, nearly as important as additional staff, and it is usually the commodity that is most difficult to find in adequate amounts. When sufficient time cannot be found within a standard work week, of course, it must be found elsewhere. In a very few cases, such as in the National Agriculture Library, some staff are given the task of developing such programs as their primary responsibility. This is true of Pamela Mason, for example, who is developing a multimedia CD-ROM-based program called Plant-It. While such a work situation is ideal, it is not absolutely essential for development of these types of programs, particularly now that the authoring and programming software is becoming easier to use and less expensive.

Updating programs can be a major impediment to the continuation of long-term interest in a project. I have found much of the excitement to be in the original development of such programs, and continuation and updating rapidly becomes drudgery. For this reason it is important that thought be given from the outset to how this can be done simply, and how such duties can be delegated to others. Scanning and downloading technologies are powerful assets in this area since they allow capturing large amounts of applicable data with relatively little work. Also, depending on databases for information storage is preferable to hard coding data into the program since a database can be modified far more easily than a program.

On balance the payback from software development has been more than adequate, both in the feeling of creativity and personal satisfaction it has provided me and in the professional contacts it has allowed me to develop within the research faculty and the library community. I also feel that such work is beneficial to the well-being of the profession as a whole and that more widespread efforts in this area will help to ensure the health and vitality of our careers into the twenty-first century.

REFERENCES

1. Wilson, David L. College enables professors to write computer programs with ease: at Allegheny, faculty members with little training quickly create sophisticated applications. *The Chronicle of Higher Education.* 38(37): A15-A16; 1992 May 20.

SYDNEY JONES
EXECUTIVE FOR OWNERS OF A NATIONAL BIBLIOGRAPHIC DATABASE

Sydney Jones is vice president, bibliographic services and customer support, at Utlas International Canada, 3300 Bloor St. West, Etobicoke, Ontario, Canada M8X 2X2. After seven years of employment at McGill University Libraries, Mr. Jones was hired in 1977 by Utlas International Canada, where he was promoted from system development librarian to manager of various departments during the period 1980 to 1989. He became a vice president in 1989 and moved to his present position in 1990. He has a B.A. from Carleton University and an M.L.S. from McGill University.

INTRODUCTION

I finished the M.L.S. program at McGill University in 1970, just as computer technology was about to be introduced to libraries. Library automation was covered in a half-course in the second year, which consisted of lectures on the MARC format and how MARC records could be built using clumsy batch applications. The potential of library databases was explored with little grounding in actual experience, and the benefits of automation were described in terms of speedy card production. Although there may have been some who had a vision of the future, I daresay that most of my colleagues viewed the course as whimsical relief in a program that emphasized the traditional values of learning reference sources and cataloging esoteric materials.

I spent the first several years as a professional in traditional library jobs: cataloger, reference librarian, and supervisor of technical processing (cards, labels, binding, and filing). I worked in an academic library at a time when the card catalog was still the only product of cataloging, when national databases consisted of compilations of catalog cards submitted to national libraries. It was a time when catalogers eagerly awaited the arrival of the next monthly issue of the *National Union Catalog* in the hope that the Library of Congress had finally cataloged some of the problem books that had been put aside as challenges too big to face.

The emergence and success of bibliographic utilities in the 1970s revolutionized technical services, and in only twenty years computer technology has insinuated its way into every type of library and every type of library job. It has also provided career opportunities unimagined by most, and has created a private sector industry that supports, develops, and markets specialized and complex products and services.

NATURE OF THE WORK

As a vice president of Canada's leading bibliographic utility, I am responsible for customer support, sales, public relations, and for the batch applications and standards that govern a database of more than sixty million bibliographic and authority records built by over four hundred customer libraries. I have had to couple the service techniques and organizational skills that are important to a successful career in librarianship with an awareness of business practice and financial objectives.

Let me start with the database. Because we are a database provider to hundreds of libraries, bibliographic standards are of the highest importance to us. Shared cataloging calls for a uniformity of record formats based on complex coding conventions. Like other utilities, Utlas purchases MARC records from a variety of sources in a number of national formats. Customers add to the files by contributing records for items cataloged originally. Reconciling formats and developing the means for libraries to enrich MARC records with local information requires a commitment to monitor and implement change, and to participate in the development of standards at the national and international levels. Utilities provide a practical voice to these discussions, since format changes often are implemented first by them. Managing change of this nature requires the full-time attention of several staff members, along with corporate recognition of the importance of this function.

The database provides excellent product opportunities beyond its principal online applications. Utlas's database specialists provide valuable advice on batch product specifications and design, as well as on the pricing components of offering these products. In order to win a retrospective conversion or authority control bid, this staff must have an understanding of competitive products and of both the company's and the customer's price concerns, and they must be able to define a project from a large number of variables. They also must be able to test, schedule, and monitor the production of many jobs simultaneously.

Every database supplier, whether in the public or private sector, must make a strong commitment to customer service. It is true that service is often the differentiating factor between organizations that offer similar products. Yet, measuring the success of service programs is one of the most difficult management functions, especially when there is a large and diversified customer base.

Frequent communication with customers is key, in the form of visits, customer update sessions, phone calls, training programs, and corporate newsletters. Monitoring the activities of selected accounts helps to gauge the overall success of an organization's communication plan. Personal contacts with key and influential customers at the executive level provide me with another measurement of the company's responsiveness to the needs and expectations of the community.

Selling services and products to the sophisticated

library market is another component of the job. The market continues to change, driven by technology, increasing client expectations, and diminishing budgets. Utlas has recently begun to establish business partnerships in order to diversify its product lines, requiring sales staff to become familiar with new products and new support networks. While sales opportunities are enhanced, the complexity of representing a broader product line requires a commitment to training and a creative understanding of customers' needs. Add to this the typically long sales cycle in the library community, and sales becomes a challenge unparalleled in most library jobs.

Finally, public relations and communications are essential marketing tools when presenting issues and plans to customers. Newsletters, conference participation, advertising, and sponsorships must be planned and executed carefully. The market is diverse and changing, and strategic communication plans require constant review and evaluation.

Of course, organizations such as Utlas employ many specialists who carry out these functions. One of the fascinating aspects of my job is the exposure to other professions that it affords. On a daily basis, I work with our chief financial officer and her accounting staff, development programmers, computer operations specialists, and marketing analysts. Some of these individuals are librarians who have sought nontraditional careers, and many are professionals in their own fields. This exposure to other professions provides a sensitivity to other disciplines not common in many library settings.

QUALIFICATIONS

I often wonder what the ideal qualifications for my job are, or should have been. Certainly, formal training in librarianship helps me to understand the nature of our customers and the products and services they require. It also helps me establish credibility with some customers, although this is no longer an issue for many. As I have already mentioned, the organizational and service skills that I learned in library school are helpful in this environment. What continue to challenge me are the business and technical skills, which are just as important. Financial reports can still mystify me. Learning to identify, analyze, prioritize, and realize opportunities from a financial perspective takes a great deal of help and advice. Would training in computer science have helped? Certainly, but learning what computers can do efficiently is even more important. Match this skill with excellent analysts and programmers, and you have the ingredients of a powerful team.

Utlas has seen many nonlibrarians succeed in sales, marketing, standards administration, and product development and support. The organization has also encouraged librarians to develop new skills and has provided appropriate training to help.

I believe that our formal training provides a solid base to diversify. I am also aware that most traditional library jobs are undergoing change, and that many of the distinctions that existed between work in libraries and work in the information industry are blurring. Librarians are installing local area networks, they are exploiting resources available locally and worldwide via telecommunications links, and they are redefining their roles in response to technological change. They are becoming information brokers, and are adding new concepts to the profession. In so doing, they will also become more aware of their need to control new kinds of costs, develop new strategies to attract patrons, and reassess traditional service measurements.

In the final analysis, while our professional goals will remain unchanged, our techniques are changing and our training is changing to reflect this. More than ever, flexibility is the key to success. Technology is a challenging competitor, and we must keep up with it.

PROS AND CONS

I remember my days as a cataloger with fondness. I can honestly say that I left my job at the office. And I was challenged every day. But technology is fun, challenging, and unavoidable; anyone choosing a career in librarianship today must come to terms with its importance. The question is whether to be a user of technology, or to be involved in its development, implementation, marketing, and support.

The choice, if made consciously, will determine the formal skills training that you seek before and during your career. The biggest advantage to working in a business setting is that it opens doors to opportunities in the information industry as a whole, and I am convinced that this sector will continue to grow and diversify. However, business skills are very important in libraries today and I feel that my fifteen years in business would in no way prevent me returning to library work again. Business and libraries both have services, customers, staff, and budgets, and the more commercial a commodity information becomes, the more libraries will adopt business practices.

NANCY KNIGHT
DIRECTOR OF PRODUCT MANAGEMENT FOR A
CD-ROM VENDOR

Nancy Knight is director of product management for academic publishing at SilverPlatter Information, Inc., 1005 N. Glebe Road, Suite 605, Arlington, VA 22201. SilverPlatter is an international corporation that publishes reference databases on CD-ROM. Ms. Knight is responsible for database acquisition and marketing of academic titles. She began her career by working for the Library Technology Program at the American Library Association, then created her own free-lance editing, indexing, and abstracting business. After twelve years in this activity, she served as a medical librarian at Georgetown University. Later she was database education specialist at the American Psychological Association, concerned with PsycLIT, APA's CD-ROM product published by SilverPlatter. Ms. Knight has a B.S. from Simmons College and an M.A. in library science from the University of Chicago. She is active in NFAIS (National Federation of Abstracting and Indexing Services), and currently chairs its Education Committee.

INTRODUCTION

Looking back, I could not have chosen a more versatile degree than my M.A. in library science from the University of Chicago. It has been a prerequisite for almost every job I've had in the past twenty-five years—and only one of them has actually been in a library!

The seeds for my career were sown by the time I was a freshman in college—I just didn't know it at the time. During high school I was a page in my small town public library—and I loved it. I decided that when I grew up, I wanted to run a public library in a suburban community. Then my horizons expanded. During the summer before college (and for four summers after that), I did editorial work on *Paperbound Books in Print*, which was published by R. R. Bowker at the time. The work was mostly clerical—editing entries for paperbound books submitted by publishing companies—but I liked the atmosphere and the content. Being an avid reader, I love knowing what books would soon be available in paperback.

My dual interest—in library science and publishing—continued through undergraduate and through graduate school. At Simmons College, I majored in the social sciences and minored in English—because I was interested in those areas, and I felt they would give me a broad background in the humanities. At the University of Chicago, my now-defunct library school, I concentrated in the public library courses. After graduation, I sought public library positions. My first interview—for a young adult position in a suburban public library—shattered my view of working in a public library. The director spent the entire interview leaping up from her chair to yell at children five and under for sticking their heads through the spindles on the staircase. Unfair as it is to generalize the entire public library field from the behavior of one director, in reality that's how decisions are made. I accepted a position in the Library Technology Program at the American Library Association (ALA) as assistant editor of *Library Technology Reports*. It combined my interest in libraries—and became pivotal for my career, which has been information industry oriented.

When my first child was born, I opted to stay at home. My contacts at ALA enabled me to begin a free-lance business in writing, indexing, editing, and abstracting primarily for the library press. I ran my own business for twelve years, and was thus able to stay in touch with the many changes in the information field. Throughout this period, my library degree gave me credibility. On the personal side, I was able to be home with my two children and relocate from Chicago to the Washington, D.C., area with virtually no interruption in my chosen career path.

Need for more outside contact and a more regular schedule motivated me to again seek work outside the home. This time I officially used my degree and accepted a position as a reference librarian at the Dahlgren Medical Library, at Georgetown University. Here I was able to hone my skills as an online searcher and expand my vision of the role of the library. Teaching faculty basic microcomputer skills and how to manage their personal reference files reinforced for me not only the importance but the necessity of information management.

When a user-education position opened up in the PsycINFO department of the American Psychological Association, I leaped at the opportunity. This time I was charged with introducing a new technology—CD-ROM—to the library market. From PsycINFO to SilverPlatter Information was a natural progression.

NATURE OF THE WORK

SilverPlatter Information, Inc., pioneered in publishing reference databases on CD-ROM. Founded in 1983 as the first company to provide information on compact disc, SilverPlatter now publishes more than one hundred CD-ROM titles.

Several years ago, SilverPlatter reorganized itself into four publishing groups to handle the acquisition, marketing, and sales of specific products. The concept behind the publishing groups was that SilverPlatter could continue to remain close to the information providers who supplied the databases and the market for these databases. Functions that cut across all publishing groups, such as database design, software development, order processing, shipping, finance, and others continue to be handled centrally. The four publishing groups include: Academic, Health Sciences, Environment, and Business. Currently, I am director of product management for the Academic Publishing Division.

The Academic Publishing Division handles titles of interest to the college and university library and large public library markets. Specifically, we publish databases that cover the basic fields of study at a college or university—psychology, sociology, economics, education, mathematics, geology, and so forth. In addition, we also publish general reference titles such as Gale's *Encyclopedia of Associations* and the *Peterson's College Database* and GRADLINE.

SilverPlatter's CD-ROM titles are sold on a subscription basis to libraries. When a library subscribes, it receives the database mastered on one or more CD-ROM discs, retrieval software on a floppy disk, and printed documentation. At regularly scheduled intervals, our subscribers receive an "update" disc, which includes all of the data on the former disc plus new data.

SilverPlatter's Information Retrieval Software (SPIRS) runs on IBM PCs and clones, the Apple Macintosh, and the NEC 9800 (Japan) machines. SilverPlatter continues to refine and enhance SPIRS to accommodate suggestions made by customers and to better present its databases. Current customers automatically receive the latest version of the software.

My primary responsibility is to develop and manage the Academic Publishing Division's titles. What that means is that I am responsible for identifying and "bringing to market" new titles, recommending and coordinating enhancements of current products, and managing relationships with our existing information providers. Further, I work with the marketing and sales groups to coordinate the marketing of these products.

In essence, my job keeps me in constant touch with information providers and librarians. Librarians' needs provide me with direction in approaching information providers. My library science degree, and my library experience—albeit limited—give me an enormous amount of credibility.

QUALIFICATIONS

The basic requirements for my position include a bachelor's degree with either an M.B.A. or M.L.S. preferred; three years of experience in product development, marketing, or user services, preferably in the information industry; and strong oral and written communication skills.

Beyond the basics, I need to have an awareness of the reference information needs of college, university, and public libraries. Also, I must be familiar with CD-ROM technology, in general, and SilverPlatter's process specifically. Knowledge of the secondary publishing business is certainly helpful in approaching potential information providers; it allows me to "talk their "language" and understand their concerns about potential migration of sales from print or online products. Finally, I need to be able to work effectively to achieve specific tasks with a multitude of people both inside and outside of SilverPlatter.

PROS AND CONS

Working for an entrepreneurial company is very different from working for a nonprofit organization, in a library or nonlibrary setting. Obviously, the bottom line is essential in a for-profit company. If it's not making a profit, it will cease to exist. But the company's goals are important, too. SilverPlatter's goal is to serve five constituents—its investors, its information providers, its customers, its staff, and society. If each is served, the company will succeed.

Many of the pros about working in an alternative library career can also be seen as cons. For me, I enjoy seeing the bottom-line results of my work. Identifying products that meet the needs of librarians and consequently brings money into the company. I find this very rewarding.

Other pros include travel—both domestic and international, opportunities to talk with many librarians and discuss their needs, attendance at multiple trade shows, an unending variety of tasks, and a competitive salary.

The cons for me are primarily confined to my lack of contact with students in a library setting. I enjoyed this part of my library work. However, for some, I could also see that travel might be a negative as well. And, of course, no one actually knows what you do—whereas, when you say you're a librarian—an image, however inaccurate, is conveyed!

FRANCES LAU
FAR EAST SALES REPRESENTATIVE FOR AN INTERNATIONAL BOOKSELLER AND PERIODICAL SUBSCRIPTION AGENCY

Frances Lau is director, library services, Far East, for Blackwell North America, Inc., 6024 S.W. Jean Road, Bldg. G, Lake Oswego, OR 97035. She was employed as a college instructor, as a reference librarian in a county library, and as a reference librarian in a university library before joining Blackwell North America in 1981 as a MARC consultant. Ms. Lau was promoted to her present position in 1983. She has a B.A. from Whitworth College and an M.L.S. from the University of Oregon. She has had several articles and book reviews published.

INTRODUCTION

Born as I was in a remote village in southern China where women of my mother's generation were commonly sold during infancy to other families as brides, concubines, or maids and were usually illiterate, it was expected of me that I would become a productive housewife and have many children when I matured.

While I was growing up I never dreamed of being a librarian, let alone a bookseller. I did have a dream then, though not an ambitious one, of making my fortune. My dream was a simple desire not to be sold as a concubine or, as in my own mother's case, a maid.

Although I am no supporter of the Communist regime in China, I am indebted to Chairman Mao Zedong for making education available to everyone, even to the girls of my village. When I was nine years old, my family and I moved to Hong Kong and settled in a village in the New Territories.

My first encounter with a "library" was a bookmobile that came to my village every Saturday morning. Although it parked only a few yards from my house, I borrowed few books because I had no spare time. After school I had to help my mother knit or crochet to earn our living, and my parents did not actively encourage us to read. My second encounter with a library was when our new high school building was opened. The library, the size of two classrooms, had only a limited number of reference books grouped by broad subjects, and most students used it as a study room anyway.

With my mother's unswerving support, I finished high school and even came to America to attend college. I wanted to become a schoolteacher. To help put myself through college, I started working in the college library part-time. My work was mainly mending damaged books. When I found out that I could not get a teaching certificate because I was not a U.S. citizen, I majored in English instead of education and minored in library science. Perhaps, I thought, I could return to Hong Kong and teach in my high school and catalog the library books!

I married on graduating from college. My husband continued in graduate school at the University of Oregon, and I remained at our alma mater to teach Chinese language and culture. A year later, I joined my husband and became a cataloger's assistant in a community college. Soon afterward I entered the University of Oregon, where I received a master's degree in library science. My first professional post was as a reference librarian at Montana State University.

When we moved to Oregon in 1981, I became a reference librarian in Portland's public library downtown. My working hours included one night a week and two weekends a month, and I had to rely on the bus for commuting, which took an hour each way on a good day.

Wanting a better family life, my husband encouraged

me to look for another job that would allow me to work regular hours. That was how I joined Blackwell North America Inc. as a part-time MARC consultant. I could still use my library education and training in a company supplying scholarly books to libraries all over the world and backing these services with technical products in many forms derived from MARC records.

My main responsibility was to upgrade Blackwell North America's own MARC records to the AACR2 format. I owe my release from this avowedly monotonous, even though important, job to President Nixon, who reestablished relations between the United States and China, and my advancement to Deng Xiaoping, who promoted the import of "the four technologies."

In the early 1980s our vice president of international sales and marketing was keen to explore the potential for our services in this emerging Chinese market. Together with the chairman of our parent company, B.H. Blackwell Limited (BHB) of Oxford, England, I went to Beijing in 1983, a visit which led to a contract worth several million dollars with the State Education Commission. My new post was director of library services, Far East, to look after our customers in this region.

NATURE OF THE WORK

My responsibilities cover a wide range. Broadly stated, they are as follows:

1.   Coordination among affiliated companies:
     I do not just look after Blackwell North America.
     I represent BHB, which sells British and
     European books and journals, and also
     Readmore, a Blackwell-owned periodical
     subscription agency located in New York and

New Jersey. As you can imagine, the coordination of this abundance of services to the benefit of my customers is an ever-stimulating challenge.

2. Sales and market development in Asian countries:
    Currently, China, Taiwan, Hong Kong and Korea fall within my territory. Opening new markets and maintaining a healthy trend of sales are my main responsibilities.

3. Business negotiations:
    Contractual or trading negotiations with customers occupy some of my time. It is generally up to me to ensure that the terms are implemented properly and that the customers' instructions are followed through by all departments concerned. When major problems occur, they often come to my desk.

4. Cooperation with local agencies:
    We have established cooperation with some local book importers or purchasing agents. It is my responsibility to maintain a good working relationship with them.

5. Presentations and seminars:
    I travel to the Far East at least twice a year. Besides giving presentations on Blackwell services on an individual basis or formally in front of a group, I am often requested to give a state-of-the-art report on American libraries. Many library directors and librarians in China do not have library or information science degrees, and, as a general rule, their libraries hardly subscribe to any Western library journals. Therefore they like to find out what is going on in Western libraries from overseas librarians.

6. Document preparation in Chinese:
    Most Chinese customers prefer writing to us in Chinese, and I often correspond in Chinese too. To make them more readily usable, I have written or translated into Chinese, with my husband's help many key Blackwell documents, such as our *User's Guide to the Blackwell Approval Plan* and *New Titles Announcement Service*, the *Blackwell Subject Thesaurus*. These activities are greatly appreciated.

QUALIFICATIONS

Raised as a Chinese, I am supposed to be modest and not boast about any success in my career. However, after living in America for more than twenty years, I could not help but adapt. So in my humble opinion, the qualifications or reasons for my success in the job as the director of library services, Far East, are as follows:

1. Qualifications:
    First of all, I am a trained librarian. I can resolve issues that are technical in nature as well as those that involve business decisions. Being able to see things from a librarian's point of view frequently helps me bridge communication between my customers and our companies. Second, I am bilingual in Chinese and English. My ability to speak both Mandarin and Cantonese has allowed me to work efficiently in China, Taiwan, and Hong Kong. Third, I am familiar with Chinese culture and customs, thus I avoid misunderstandings that could cause embarrassment, yet I make it easier to build up trust and friendship with my customers.

2. Gratifying relationships with satisfied customers:
    To see a smiling customer who is happy with our
    services helps me forget the stress of reaching
    this rewarding stage. Once trust is established,
    many customers treat me as a personal friend.
    Some librarians even invite me home for dinner.
    I am always touched by the fact that they, along
    with their families, go to so much trouble to
    prepare a sumptuous meal (ten courses or more
    are quite common) at their own expense on
    inadequate salaries to welcome me.

3. Support from my superiors:
    My greatest mentors at work are the chairman of
    BHB and the vice president of international sales
    and marketing at Blackwell North America. The
    former gave me my first-hand training and
    guidance when we visited China together for the
    first few years. He taught me that integrity,
    devotion to the customers, and dedication to
    work are far more important than just making a
    profit. The latter, an intelligent and hard-working
    man also, has recognized my abilities and special
    skills. He helps me in reaching my potential.
    With an excellent understanding of library needs
    and remarkable foresight, both superiors give me
    invaluable advice.

4. Cooperation from my colleagues:
    My colleagues at Blackwell North America,
    BHB, and Readmore, are friendly and helpful. I
    can always count on their cooperation. Our
    common goal is to render good service to our
    customers. When a problem occurs, we dig into
    the core to find out the source and correct it. As
    a team, we share the successes. We are willing to
    go out of our way to satisfy our customers, as in
    the case of providing Chinese versions of key
    documents.

5. Support from my husband:
    My husband is a Chinese consultant and a
    scholar with the gift of being able to write in
    beautiful calligraphy, and he possesses
    extraordinary skills in desktop publishing.
    Besides offering his continual encouragement and
    mental support, he also helps me with my work
    as I have already mentioned. Many of the
    translated documents were either handwritten or
    typeset by him.

6. Gratitude to loved ones:
    My desire not to disappoint those who love and
    support me is a driving force to perform well. I
    am most indebted to my mother, because
    although she had a miserable childhood and is
    illiterate herself, she saw to it that I finished high
    school and then went to America to receive a
    college education. I am also grateful to my
    "American grandma" and my "American parents"
    for their encouragement and help. There are high
    school teachers, college professors, and friends,
    and the dean of women at Whitworth College
    whose kindness I can never forget.

THE PROS AND CONS

I love my job because I can make full use of my
education and training in library science as well as my
cultural background. I also like the variety of my
responsibilities. Although I did not become a teacher as
originally planned, I do have chances to give seminars and
presentations. I enjoy visiting with librarians and meeting
potential customers. My job is challenging because library
requirements and needs change all the time. When I am not
traveling on business or entertaining foreign visitors, I can

stay home in the evenings or on weekends. In other words, when I am in town, I have more or less regular working hours.

The single biggest drawback is the process of traveling. Contrary to popular belief, business traveling is not glamorous. True, the company pays for my work-related travel expenses, but because of the great distance between the Far East and America, I have to make good use of my trips. Therefore, I am away at least four weeks each time, and at least twice a year. Imagine how much yard work and housework I skip during each spring and fall! Before a trip, there are many chores both in the office and at home to finish, and upon my return, there is always a backlog to catch up on. When I am overseas, I usually work long hours—at least two customer visits per day, and report writing in the evening. In China, I visit libraries six days a week and try to travel from city to city on Sundays. Homesickness is a common phenomenon and rejections from potential customers can be disheartening.

Currently, my career path in the company lies through the Vice-President to whom I report, but I do not have his depth and breadth of experience with many other countries. In the short term my job keeps me more than busy, and I have the regard of my customers and peers. Not even the prospect of returning to Hong Kong to profit from the opportunities before and after 1997 has tempted my husband and me, nor could I think of working with a lesser company here or elsewhere.

To sum up, to be a bookseller requires dedication, integrity, and a good relationship with both customers and colleagues. The job requires extensive traveling, and, if you travel to the Orient, a strong stomach for exotic food such as snake soups, duck feet, and sea cucumbers. It also provides good career opportunities and the job is relatively secure. The salaries vary from one company to another, but on the whole, are somewhat higher than those of traditional librarians. If you are interested in becoming a bookseller, please be sure to visit a book vendor to see for yourself.

PEGGY MARTIN
DIRECTOR OF MANAGEMENT INFORMATION SYSTEMS (MIS) AT A LARGE LAW FIRM

Peggy Martin is director of management information systems at Mudge Rose Guthrie Alexander & Ferdon, 180 Maiden Lane, New York, NY 10038. She has been employed in law firms since 1974, joining the library staff of her present employer in 1983. She has also served as a consultant to private and government clients. Ms. Martin has been active in many library organizations, particularly the Law Library Association of Greater New York (LLAGNY), serving in several capacities, including its presidency in 1983-1984. She received a B.A. from Connecticut College, an M.S. from Columbia University School of Library Service, an M.B.A. degree from New York University, and certification from the American Association of Law Librarians in 1981.

INTRODUCTION

The position of management information systems (MIS) director is relatively new in large law firms. It emerged in the mid-1980s as an amalgam of functions formerly handled by individual departments. The functions included under the title vary significantly from firm to firm. At Mudge Rose, where I am the director of MIS, the functions grouped under this title are library, records, data processing, word processing, facsimile, telephones and most recently, local area network (LAN).

I was promoted into the position on January 1, 1986. Prior to my tenure, the functions, with the exception of the library and records center, were under the direction of the firm's controller. I had been managing the library and records center and was asked to continue with these departments in addition to the more traditional IS departments.

In many firms the position is filled by a former manager of the computer room (or data processing facility) or by the firm's telecommunications guru. However, Mudge Rose regarded my background in librarianship as an important foundation for directing the IS operations at the firm.

Through my background in librarianship, I had a working knowledge of how to organize information, both printed and electronic. My experience with online database searching prepared me for understanding database design and structure and database search logic. The importance of this experience cannot be overestimated since the word-processing system in a law firm is really a large database of the firm's documents, and the firm's financial accounting package is a large database of the firm's financial history.

I arrived at Mudge Rose in 1983 with the specific mandate to acquire law materials to round out the collection and move that collection to the firm's new location seven months later. In 1985, I volunteered to oversee the records center, believing that the records function was an extension of librarianship insofar as it was organizing, indexing, and locating information. In 1986, the concept of information management was expanded to include electronic systems as well as manual systems, hence the name management information systems.

NATURE OF THE WORK

The nature of any job in a law firm revolves around an understanding of the singular corporate culture of law firms. Law firms are partnerships, governed by a hierarchical structure of committees. At any given time, each partner is your "boss." This means that you must literally please each partner all the time. Exceptions are the rule, standardization is a recommendation at best, and service (providing each and every partner with what he or she wants) is paramount. It is also wise to remember that service is not just what the partner requests; it is requested for the client, by the client, because of the client.

In fact, lawyers and clients are not a department's only customers. Other departments might also be your client. For example, the accounting department is data processing's client. Data processing houses the computer that runs accounting's financial software and the programmers who write the code to enhance that software. The human resources department is the records center's clients. Records houses and manages the incoming and outgoing records of these departments, as well as the lawyer's legal files. Administration is the library's client. The library does many research projects for administration for practice/client development purposes.

Another hallmark of law firm culture is the expected standard of excellence. In the daily life of the firm, this translates into a requirement for excellence in quality *and* quantity. There is seldom adequate time to complete the task. Rather, there is a constant juggling of priorities to complete the task as well as possible and as quickly as possible. Request interviews and close follow-up are not just the domain of the library staff; they are required of every department's staff.

Within this environment, the duties and opportunities of the MIS director are infinite. However, the prime directive is simple and straightforward: keep the systems running. We keep the systems running twenty-four hours a day, seven days a week. Downtime, except for system backups, is unacceptable.

The MIS director's duties fall into three categories:

staff management, budget creation and monitoring, and technical knowledge. Each department reporting to me is headed by a manager. I am responsible for hiring and evaluating each of these managers.

On a daily basis, I listen to each manager's reports, and track the projects on which each is working. I query managers regarding delayed projects and status of current tasks. Many projects are of a crisis nature, meaning that other tasks are temporarily dropped while the crisis is resolved. I track project progress to ensure that deadlines are met. For example, a tape drive might fail on the accounting system's computer. Since the tape drive is used nightly during the production phase, the vendor must be called immediately; if necessary, parts must be shipped in overnight and equipment repaired within no more than twenty-four hours. The data processing manager must monitor this process and work with the vendor for a speedy resolution of the problem. Usually, a memorandum describing the problem and the steps taken to resolve it is prepared by the manager upon resolution of the problem. Then, the manager and I must confer and reestablish priorities to bring previous projects back online.

Each manager is responsible for the creation and monitoring of his or her department's expense budget, with quarterly reports to me on the variance between actual amounts spent and budgeted amounts. I then meet with accounting and the executive director, to whom I report, and explain variances. A report is generated and presented to the executive committee.

Each manager is expected to be the technical expert for his or her department. My role is one of translator. The manager describes technical problems to me, and I must rephrase the problem for the lawyers and the executive director. For example, if changes to a document are saved onto the LAN, I must understand the nature of the system, or Btrieve error, and explain it briefly in general, lay terms. The more important part of my explanation tells the lawyer *when* the system will be back to normal, as opposed to why the problem occurred. If the records center cannot locate a file, I must explain all the steps taken to track it down with a suggestion as to what might have happened to the file. If the telephones are not being answered on a timely basis, I must investigate the reasons and relay these as well as the steps being taken to avoid the situation in the future.

In some instances, the manager and I work with one of the firm's committees. This is the case with the LAN, which is currently being installed. The manager and I meet weekly with the Automation Committee to discuss issues ranging from software selection and upgrades to contracts or scope of work with the vendor installing the new system.

The greatest opportunity in the area of MIS is the opportunity to learn about new technologies as they enter the marketplace. The connectivity issues and data communication capabilities of the local area network world are being implemented as they are developed. At Mudge Rose, we have opted to work in the Windows environment. Although increasing numbers of software applications are available in Windows, we still have to connect to the DOS world through Windows. In the area of telecommunications, we are exploring voice mail alternatives and videoconferencing. The library is expanding the collection into the CD-ROM media, which is less expensive and saves space. We expect to have access to the CD-ROM libraries available on the network in late 1992. The firm is also using optical disk storage for the full text of depositions and trial transcripts.

QUALIFICATIONS

I have gotten a 100 percent return on my investment in library school. In addition to the master's degree in library service, I hold a master's in business administration. While the M.B.A. is certainly useful in solving managerial, accounting, and financial problems, it does not affect my daily skills as directly as the M.L.S. The M.L.S. gives me an understanding of service and organizational expectations that I apply every day.

Several law librarians have gone to law school to enhance their skills as law librarians or to prepare themselves for teaching legal research, ethics, or other courses. In fact, most law schools now require both the M.L.S. and J.D. for reference librarian and head librarian positions. However, the J.D. is not essential for the law firm librarian who has a good grasp of legal literature and lawyer expectations. In a law firm, any collateral assignments are likely to be offered based on the librarian's document organization skill.

The MIS profession is not yet as rich in its continuing education offerings as the library profession. The professional associations, through which continuing education courses are typically offered, are less prevalent. Those that do exist are well-attended. For example, Legal Tech is a technology event held annually in New York City and on the west coast. Both the vendor exhibits and workshops are informative on emerging technologies. Vendors are another excellent source of education on new technology. Lotus holds half-day seminars upon release of major new versions of its products. This fall Lotus presented its Windows versions of 1-2-3, Ami Pro, and Freelance. It is also currently holding half-day seminars on Lotus Notes. In addition to shows and vendor presentations, the value of current reading cannot be underestimated for exposure to new products and technologies. Finally, there is trial and error on the job, which may be painful but is real experiential learning.

The ultimate source for learning about the quality of the service you are providing is user feedback. Recently, with the advent of the total quality management concept in law firms, the lawyers *and* nonlegal staff have been surveyed for their view of how all of the administrative departments are running. With the survey collated, managers and directors at the firm will embark on a continuing campaign to improve service via fine-tuned procedures and attitudes.

Although technical knowledge is absolutely necessary, the managerial skills of the MIS director make or break the position for the firm. The director must be able to organize large quantities of work, and handle crises calmly. The director must have superb people skills to successfully orchestrate the large volume of work. I have found experience to be the best teacher in these areas; however, the courage of your convictions can be gained through conferences with colleagues both within and outside the firm. Also, the American Management Association offers several seminars on management techniques.

PROS AND CONS

The rewards in MIS work are as numerous as the duties and opportunities described above. In MIS, proposed projects are undertaken and completed. Watching the myriad pieces fit (or fall!) together, is compelling. The pieces are generally ideas, equipment, and applications you have personally introduced and learned about as the project evolved. I find it very rewarding to have tangible evidence of my work and to have the work benefit the user community.

Personally, I thoroughly enjoy the people I come into contact with during the course of a given project or task. The vendor aspect alone brings me into contact with hundreds of people representing different aspects or approaches to the work.

Being on the leading edge of computer technology and watching it develop is a unique experience. Although I started in MIS with a solid understanding of database structure, there have been several new aspects to learn about; including the ways in which different programming languages are applied, or the how application software acts in a particular hardware environment.

The chance to learn new software packages for improved job performance is always welcome, such as Lotus 1-2-3 for number crunching or software for project management. Using WordPerfect to compose reports at the keyboard has changed the way I create a document. Exposure to electronic mail has revealed an entire new method of communicating, in addition to the phone and interoffice memoranda. E-mail is right at hand for those fleeting ideas you want to pass on to a staff member who is not at his or her desk.

The primary disadvantage of MIS in a law firm is that some of the lawyers know more about applications than either my staff or I. There is a cadre of lawyers in every firm who are computer hobbyists. This is a somewhat precarious situation but also inevitable since the range of data to be absorbed in any given week is enormous. A second disadvantage is that not everyone understands my position. It is a constant challenge to convey what I do in an understandable way.

However, the primary task in MIS, as in any profession, is to turn frustrations into challenges. This, in itself, is the greatest challenge and requires the most creativity. I think the MIS field is an exciting alternative for energetic, service-minded, and receptive librarians.

WILDA B. NEWMAN
INFORMATION SPECIALIST AS A CHANGE AGENT AT A RESEARCH AND DEVELOPMENT LABORATORY

Wilda B. Newman is information resources manager for the Administrative Services Department (ASD) at The Johns Hopkins University, Applied Physics Laboratory, Bld. 7, Room 278, Laurel, MD 20723-6099. She was employed for sixteen years in various positions at the laboratory, including working with translations, interlibrary loans, and library management. Then eight years ago she began a new career at her present position in the area of information management. Ms. Newman has a B.S. in business administration from the University of Maryland and an M.L.S. from Catholic University. She is active in the Special Libraries Association, serving as chair and treasurer of the Science-Technology Division and advertising manager for *Sci-Tech News*; she was recently appointed chair of the association's International Relations Committee. She is also active in the International Federation of Library Associations and Institutions (IFLA) as an elected member of the Standing Committee on Information Technology.

INTRODUCTION

I am just completing my tenth year as an information specialist for the Administrative Services Department (ASD) at The Johns Hopkins University, Applied Physics Laboratory. In this capacity my duties have required among other things, that I function more and more as a Change Agent.

After sixteen years of library experience, which included work in translations, interlibrary loans, reference, supervision of acquisitions and technical services, and library management, I embarked on a different career, using my library skills and expertise. This area of information management required evaluation of organizational publications, management, coordination, and publication of the organizations' manual for practices and procedures, and, over the last eight years, management and coordination of computing for the department as an information resources manager.

Change embodies transformation—making something different from what it was, and the agent is the person or representative who causes that change or transformation. Special librarians are particularly suited to becoming change agents because they work with all types of information and its coupling with today's technology. Cortez (1) says that the Special Library Association's motto, "putting knowledge to work," is the same philosophy that is at the root of what today is called information resources management (IRM). He goes on to state, "IRM is seen as a dynamic process of managing discrete pieces of information for the purpose of helping individuals and/or organizations meet their mission. IRM views information as an organizational resource with intrinsic value. An early and firm foundation in IRM has characterized the development of special librarianship for over 50 years. It has given the special library group a professional identity which has distinguished it from other types of librarians."

It is this uniqueness that especially qualifies the special librarian to perform as a change agent. Most special librarians spend their library careers coping with change within their organizations, often brought on by the effects of outside forces. Computer technology represents the single most important of these changes. Numerous special libraries used their organizations' mainframe computer systems decades ago to harness their capability, and applied that to coping with major information management and retrieval problems. This decade has broadened many of these experiences to include librarians from other types of libraries and this trend will undoubtedly continue. In fact, fewer traditional jobs that take advantage of only a library degree as we know it today may be available in the future. Cronin (2) indicates that the postindustrial society displaced the work force from labor-intensive extractive and manufacturing industries to service and information-related industries. I would suggest that as these changes in the work force continue, librarians will suffer a similar displacement, unless they are given additional education to complement the traditional core library requirements. This is necessary if librarians are to function as meaningful change agents now, and more important, in the coming years as libraries and information science continue their transformation based on the use of computer technology. Acton (3) indicates that a wide range of management, technical, and administrative skills are needed for the challenging work that requires all the tools provided by current information theory and technology. Furthermore, this is not seen as outside the mainstream for today's librarians, when in the past this would have meant librarians who work outside traditional libraries. Burnham-Kidwell (4) considers library skills eminently transferable.

The changes we see, experience, and even promote in our profession are not limited to the United States. Jackson (5) discusses the librarian's social role, Cronin (6) looks at information and productivity relative to information technology, while Bischoff-Kuemmel (7) notes that "...those who found posts in areas outside librarianship rarely returned to it." The use of technology in planning, organizing, and managing information has resulted in public recognition of librarians, offering greater career opportunities, according to Baskin. (8)

NATURE OF THE WORK

For the past several years my main duty has been to transform the work in ASD from manual operations to automated systems, including the use of mainframe and personal computers. This work involves management and coordination of computing activities, including policy, strategic and operations plans, development, operational issues assessment, and allocation of resources. Furthermore, I develop and manage the department computing budget for applications development, software, hardware, and personnel. I also coordinate and manage the ASD database activity, both new and ongoing, through development, implementation, and maintenance. There are currently some thirty databases in operation, others under development, and still others being replaced by even newer technology. I must also ensure ASD standards for operating procedures, software, and hardware in the continuing development of automation of the department functions.

My duties are not limited to my department, either. I am often called on to participate in special committees, both as a member and as chair of the process action teams (PAT) under total quality, and as a representative of my department on a laboratory-wide basis for computing and associated information management issues. One such activity has been the APL Management and Business Systems Program (AMBSP) which began Phase II of its effort in 1990, and has continued through 1991 with work involving accounts payable, core accounting, contract administration, human resources, and procurement. In this program I perform as an applications manager of the equipment and supplies area, under the AMBS program, now referred to as the modernization effort (ME) across the organization. This activity is continuing in 1992 and beyond.

In 1991 examples of my related work on AMBSP included a review of software products for the organization's management of government property and calibration and procurement of these packages. I am currently managing implementation of this system. In addition, as a member of the Core Accounting and Procurement Selection Evaluation Board, I was involved in the review and evaluation of products that led to the purchase of business applications software for the Business and Information Services Department.

I also provide oversight and management for the project to convert the Document Record Center and Security operations to the DEC/VAX environment from the IBM/MVS and IBM/VM platform. These applications will be using purchased applications software, under the AMBSP Security Applications Area.

In addition, other examples of my recent work, include membership in the AMBSP Network Implementation Ad Hoc Networking Group, and its "Tiger Team" on Programmatic Issues; draft of a policy memo on the laboratory computing users group; and consultant to the laboratory's recreational organization's cafeteria operations on the automation of food services. More recently, I am reviewing business issues that result from our extensive transformation of the laboratory's business and management information systems. Also associated with my work is the planning, management, and implementation of an ASD network, for which I am responsible.

With this background let me use two very specific examples of how, as change agent, library and information science skills are used by an information resources manager. Two projects, property and calibration, and the document record center (DRC) are under conversion.

The property and calibration system will use a catalog of equipment. Currently, the automated system enters a separate description for every item, even if there are fifty or more of the same item. The new system will eliminate this duplication. In addition, the new catalog will allow more efficient retrieval and better use of property/equipment and associated resources, since it will rely on entry standardization. The catalog was purchased as part of the software, and the software vendor offers a conversion service. Justification for the use of these conversion services was partially based on book cataloging costs obtained from the Library of Congress.

The DRC system tracks technical reports classified as secret. The old system has many of the same problems as the property and calibration system, even though it should not include duplication of entries that are associated with different DRC numbers, according to Defense Investigative Services (DIS) requirements. The data are not standardized, nor do they lend themselves to efficient retrieval and management. We are currently working with the Defense Technical Information Center (DTIC) to determine whether it might be able to assist us with data conversion and cleanup of the bibliographic records in the DRC system.

In both cases the underlying basic requirements for data entry and data integrity are of paramount importance. The special librarian has the requisite information knowledge and skills to ensure at basic information data structures permit proper selection, acquisition, organization, retrieval, and dissemination of information.

Professional work outside the organization has also continued at both the national and international level. Besides my active participation in the Special Libraries Association, I am completing my fourth year as an elected member to the Standing Committee on Information Technology of the International Federation of Library Associations and Institutions (IFLA). And, as part of this effort I worked on a proposal (which has been funded) on graphical user interfaces (GUI) for end-user computing. This is an area of particular interest to the laboratory's AMBSP, as is development of a common user interface for delivery of laboratory management and business information.

I mention the professional work outside the organization to indicate a commitment to the library and information science profession, but also to remind others of our profession, especially those working outside the traditional "library," to review their own work relative to specific skills they use and to acknowledge these skills as necessary and required by their degree in library and information science. In addition, as professionals we must be willing to give back to our profession if it is to survive and grow. Librarianship is becoming even more tightly integrated with computer technology; we need to acknowledge the change in requirements necessary for our future use this change to broaden the public's understanding of our profession.

QUALIFICATIONS

Reflection on my career prompts an assessment of the qualifications necessary to perform as change agent in an information resources management position. There is no question that the foremost qualification is service to the end user, no matter how end user is defined. Many technologists are most taken with the technology, and even in our own profession of librarianship there are those who are more concerned with putting the knowledge on the shelf, so to speak, as opposed to putting it to work. As change agent my goal is to put the knowledge to work, not only for the functional support group (end users), but for those who need access to it for decision making and reporting outside the group (end users). Too often systems are defined and designed only to get a job done more efficiently, and not to serve the whole more effectively, rather than just the caretaker of the data. When *all* users of that information are enlisted, they are *all equally important* relative to retrieval of the data they need and use as information.

The traditional library core requirements are not enough for the professional librarian of the future. Gluckman (9) sees pressure from the marketplace as the force to bring about more changes in the education of information professionals. He suggests that programs in information processing take up where librarianship leaves off. There is also the argument in the information profession over boundary lines. Knoppers (10) suggests that information professionals should join forces and educate top management. It is also noted that an interdisciplinary approach is required for information management. Slater (11) sums it up best: "...more consideration should be given to the future role of a unified profession in a fast changing world."

PROS AND CONS

A retrospective of my "library" career and my continuing work as an information specialist has been challenging and rewarding. Certainly the change has broadened my responsibilities, promoted my knowledge base, and encouraged continuing education in all of the fields that I believe are so necessary for the future information specialist, formerly librarian, for success in the decades ahead. Furthermore, the change has allowed me to work in areas and at levels of information and systems management not as accessible in a typical "special library" setting. And it has allowed me to demonstrate the librarian's capabilities that are valuable and relate to a variety of information management assignments.

The main disadvantage in my current career is that most people define a librarian as a person in charge of or trained for work in a library. Most people are not aware of what it takes to become a skilled information specialist (my preferred term) Even the term special librarian requires people to comment, "I thought all librarians were special." Not a bad thought, but it misses the point. Even the work I continue to do in the library and information science profession elicits such comments as, "Oh, are you *still* involved with those groups?" as if I should have escaped by now and affiliated with some other professional body, as if these professional associations must be mutually exclusive.

I could, of course, join the computer societies, management associations, and others, for example. The point is, I am not, nor do I desire to be thought of as, a technologist or manager first and an information provider second. In fact, I am all of these as an information resources manager, by education, training, and experience. And as such I operate as a change agent, hoping first to do no harm in my practice, but, rather to bring quality and effectiveness to the information systems I manage, and assistance to the people I serve as end users in their goals and mine, to help individuals and organizations meet their missions.

References

1. Cortez, Edwin M. Developments in special library education: implication for the present and future. *Special Libraries.* 77(4): 198–206; 1986 Fall.

2. Cronin, Blaise. Post industrial society: some manpower issues for the library/information profession. *Journal of Information Science.* 7(1): 1–14; 1983 August.

3. Acton, Patricia. Alternative careers? *Canadian Library Journal.* 43(6): 385–387; 1986 December.

4. Burnham-Kidwell, Debbie. Librarians without libraries. *Community and Junior College Libraries.* 3(3): 5–8; 1985 Spring.

5. Jackson, Miles M. The social role of librarians. *Figi Library Association.* (1): 13–22; 1979 August.

6. Cronin B. Information research and productivity.

Information Technology and Information Use: Towards a United View of Information and Information Technology. Conference held 8–10 May 1985, Copenhagen, Denmark; 1986; p. 11–23. Edited by P. Ingwersen, L. Kajberg, and A. M. Pejtersen. London; Taylor Graham; 1988.

7. Bischoff-Kuemmel, Gudrun; Feller, Antje. Career entry and progress by female librarians; an investigation of graduates from Hamburg Library School. *Bibliotheksdienst.* 23(4): 369–380; 1989.

8. Baskin, Judith. The new information professionals in Australia. *COMLA Newsletter.* (56): 8–9; 1987 June.

9. Gluckman, Paul. Educating the information manager. *Information Manager.* 1(1): 30–31; 1978 August.

10. Knoppers, J. Integrating technologies—integrating disciplines? *Records Management Quarterly.* 17(1): 5–7, 26; 1983 January.

11. Slater, Margaret. Alternative careers for library-information workers. *ASLIB Proceedings.* 36(6): 277–286; 1984 June.

JOHN J. REGAZZI
EXECUTIVE IN A PUBLISHING FIRM OFFERING PRINT AND COMPUTER-BASED INFORMATION SERVICES

John J. Regazzi is president and CEO of Engineering Information Inc., Castle Point on the Hudson, Hoboken, NJ 07030. He was involved with information systems at two universities and at the Foundation Center in New York City before serving as a vice president of the H.W. Wilson Company, from 1981 to 1988. In 1988 he was appointed to his present position at Engineering Information Inc. He has a B.A. from St. John's University, an M.A. from the University of Iowa, an M.S. from Columbia University's School of Library Service, and the Ph.D. from Rutgers University's School of Communication, Information Studies, Journalism and Library Science.

INTRODUCTION

Tomorrow's researcher or executive will be able to seek information independent of space and time. If, for example, you find yourself thirty-five thousand feet above Tokyo in an airplane, or on a commuter train outside of Chicago, and you want to send a voice message, document, or even a video image to your office in New York, your task will be simple. The computer chip on your cufflinks or bracelet will set the process in motion and will also be able to receive in an instant a response or a copy of a research paper or file you may wish to consult right away. All records will be digitized, online, and available twenty-four hours a day from anywhere in the world. This access and flexibility is perhaps the greatest benefit that communications and information technologies bring our present age and the next century. The empowerment of tomorrow's workers with these technologies will dwarf any of today's technologies. The fax machine, for example, will appear as quaint in the future as the manual typewriter does to us today.

Ei, the organization in which I serve as chief executive, will supply information services to those researchers and executives of tomorrow. Perhaps more important, Ei will need to compete with a myriad other information services wishing to meet the demands and needs of these sophisticated and discerning clients. This environment will not be for the faint of heart, and I suspect that the qualifications of most chief executives of these information services companies will be very different in a very few years from what they are today. Past is neither prologue nor predictive of future needs. These rapidly changing capabilities, however, will provide those who can discern unique opportunities with the ability to move quickly and to achieve potentially marvelous results both for their companies and their own careers.

NATURE OF THE WORK

Engineering Information Incorporated

What is Engineering Information Inc.? **An international information service.** Engineering Information Inc. (Ei) is the answer to the question, "Where can I find reliable information on today's technological breakthroughs?" Now in its second century of providing researchers with the right answers, Ei is the most comprehensive, centralized source of engineering information in the world. This independent, nonprofit service is dedicated to disseminating technical and scientific knowledge to the international community of engineers, technical and product information specialists, managers, and educators.

Ei's efforts include indexing and descriptive abstracting of articles, papers, and products in thousands of research and technical journals and conference series covering all engineering disciplines, originating in over forty countries worldwide. Ei's print and electronic publications are often the first place technical managers or graduate students in need of a formative first glimpse of a new technology look, as do seasoned R&D specialists seeking comprehensive information or a reliable second opinion. And in many cases, Ei is the only place engineers can turn to for access to this material. Its production of *Engineering Index* (a printed index), and COMPENDEX (its online database) has made Ei internationally known.

A Not-for-Profit Publisher—And More

Because Ei is a not-for-profit publisher, its products, services, or policies are not determined only by the bottom line, but rather by the needs, capabilities, and resources of its clients. Ei provides its data in the full complement of print, microform, and electronic formats designed to be useful, accessible, and affordable for the largest potential audience. But publishing is just a part of it. Ei has long been at the forefront of information science research and development, investigating new information dissemination technologies, exploring appropriate formats, and supporting any new initiatives with a comprehensive training and user assistance program to ensure maximum benefits.

A Unique Communications Link

In the final analysis, Ei is a necessity. Ei is the only organization dedicated to creating, maintaining, and preserving the vital, tenuous chain of communication among scientists, engineers, and consumers. At a time of worldwide concern over scientific illiteracy and the decline of education standards, when the accelerating evolution of new technology is outpaced by society's need for its application, Ei is the only discipline-based information link that joins the lab in New Mexico, the corporate information center in New York, and the university library reference room in New Delhi.

QUALIFICATIONS

When I first joined Ei nearly four years ago, it was part of an industry generally described as the "abstracting and indexing" industry, and in fact, in our own corporate culture, we considered ourselves to be in the "abstracting and indexing" business. This view, though deadly for the future, was natural enough for the time. Most of us came from organizations whose main functions and historical roots were to organize a literature or discipline, such as engineering, chemistry, biology, psychology, medicine, and so forth, by abstracting and indexing the journals in those fields of study.

I "grew up" in this industry under the leadership of two "bosses" to whom I am deeply indebted for what they taught me firsthand. I worked at the Foundation Center, a not-for-profit information services company that provided information about private foundations and their grant-giving activities, for nearly four years under Thomas R. Buckman, then the center's president. I also worked for nearly eight years at The H.W. Wilson Company under Leo M. Weins, who has been president of the company, now for nearly 30 years. Both of these men stressed three things in publishing: QUALITY, QUALITY, QUALITY. There were other issues, but I left both of these organizations with the view that high-quality service was both a professional responsibility and a competitive advantage. Tom and Leo also shared some values that I believe are essential for tomorrow's executives. These include some basic and rather commonsense approaches to our business, which can be easily overlooked in today's changing and complex information world. These are: (1) understand the market needs and think broadly about these needs; (2) find efficiencies and competitive advantages in the application of technology; (3) take calculated risks in order to do something new and preemptive; and (4), (5), (6) CONTROL COSTS, CONTROL COSTS, CONTROL COSTS. I could tell you a few stories about Tom and Leo that might entertain and enlighten your sense of this business, but there is one, in particular, involving Leo which illustrates some of the personal qualifications it takes to be successful in this business.

While at the Wilson Company, I was responsible for computer services. We were automating each editorial unit, while also developing WILSONLINE, WILSEARCH, and WILSONDISC, the electronic services of the company. As a result, we were constantly monitoring our computer capacity, and in 1985 we had reached a point where we needed to make a major decision regarding our next computer upgrade. This decision involved more than a million dollars in expenditures over a relatively short period of time. We had a plethora of financial models and capacity models, and we had analyzed the price-performance benefits of all of the appropriate existing models on the market. At the time we were running an IBM 4381, but we needed about twice that capacity. IBM, Amdhal, and others were proposing upgrading their top-end machines, but IBM offered a significant discount if we signed within thirty days. The discount was worth about $100,000 as I recollect. One day while in the computer room, Wilson's director of systems programming called me over to our 4381 machine, which was open and undergoing maintenance at the time. He asked me what I saw, and thinking this could only be a prank, I told him a lot of boards and a lot of space. He replied "exactly"—pointing out that the boards were all on the left side of this machine, while the other half was completely empty. The significance of this was that IBM had obviously designed this machine to hold two computers—i.e., a dual processor—and this would be a much more cost-effective solution than any machine on the market if it were available. Although there were some industry rumors that IBM would offer such an option, IBM was not committing to it; in fact, its sales force said they knew of no such plans. (I believe the IBM sales force was the last to know.)

Well, our choices were clear: sign up in about seven days with IBM's discount of $100,000, or lose the discount in the hopes of saving perhaps five to ten times that over the life of the machine. I told Leo I thought we should wait. He was a little surprised and more than a little skeptical, particularly when I told him why—that our present box was "half empty." For whatever reason, and it is not entirely clear to me to this day, Leo agreed. IBM was shocked, and thought we were nuts. The wait was interminable.

About two months later, during which I could stop hallway conversations by merely walking by, I was in Denver when I got a call that IBM announced the 4381-model 2—a dual processor upgrade available immediately. Industry analysts were proclaiming it the best-priced performance machine in the IBM line. I told Leo and in retrospect I believe it was dumb luck. But in the process, Leo illustrated, one of the most important characteristics of a CEO—you need to be willing to play poker on occasion. In fact, understanding the nature of this business and when to take risks is something a Leo Weins or Tom Buckman has developed over a long period, and no amount of modeling will ever replace it. (And as noted, a certain amount of dumb luck helps as well.)

THE PROS AND CONS

The Bad News

It's a rainy Sunday morning, and I am writing this article in the San Francisco airport. I live in New York; I left home on Wednesday and will not return for another week. That's not meant to be a complaint—it's just the reality of working in a midsize not-for-profit company. Most of the work in such a company gets done by a few; if you like regular hours, this career is not for you. I left my eldest son studying for an English final in which he needed some help on understanding gerunds, and I hope I can help him over the telephone later today (I'm the family gerund expert). One of my other sons had a diving meet in Connecticut in which he wanted to compete, but with me out of town it had to be scrapped. These aren't complaints either. If anyone should complain, it's my family; they don't, but rightfully they could. These realities are much harsher than the irregular hours, and they require much more serious consideration.

The Good News

If you have an idea about how the world might be better informed, and you think you can make it happen—running a small to midsize information services company is the right organization to be in. The size and the nature of such a company permits you and your colleagues to make a difference. In this environment, a good idea reigns supreme. Nothing will cut through the budget cycle, or the program priority list, faster than a good idea; an organization of this size can make good ideas a reality—and quickly too.

Perhaps the best news I can conclude with is to tell you that this job lets you find and hire good people to help you. If there is any one key to success—it's good people. At Ei, there are about fifty of us, and as we noted many times, we're only "one deep" in every position. We have no "belts and suspenders" situations—and that is another reality of this environment. Small staffs working together, however, provide an opportunity to foster and realize some of the best working relationships and friendships I have ever known.

JAMES E. RUSH, MERYL CINNAMON AND JEANNE-ELIZABETH COMBS EXECUTIVE AND MANAGERS IN A LIBRARY NETWORK

James E. Rush is executive director of PALINET, 3401 Market Street, Suite 262, Philadelphia, PA 19104-3374. From 1968 to 1973 he was associate professor of computer and information science at Ohio State University, after serving in both editorial and management capacities at the Chemical Abstracts Service (1962-68). From 1973 to 1980 he was director of research and development at OCLC while serving as an adjunct professor at both Ohio State University and University of Illinois (Urbana). He joined PALINET in 1988 after serving for eight years as president of James E. Rush Associates, Inc., a consulting firm. He has a B.S. in chemistry and mathematics from Central Missouri State University and Ph.D. in organic chemistry from the University of Missouri (Columbia). He has coauthored two books on information science and edited an eight-volume set of guides to library system evaluation. He has written scores of articles on computer, library, and information science.

Meryl Cinnamon is manager, OCLC services department at PALINET. Prior to this, she was coordinator of network services, PALINET (1987–1989); marketing representative, Chadwyck-Healey Inc., Alexandria, Virginia (1987); manager, marketing support, Utlas International U.S. Inc., Arlington, Virginia (1986–1987); manager of member services, CAPCON Library Network, Washington, D.C. (1985–1986); library network coordinator, CAPCON Library Network (1983–1985), and head catalog librarian for music/AV, Rutgers University Libraries (1979-1983). She has a BA from Rutgers College, Rutgers University, and an M.L.S. from the Graduate School of Library and Information Studies, Rutgers University.

Jeanne-Elizabeth Combs is coordinator, database services, at PALINET. Her previous positions include cataloger, reference librarian, special librarian, automation consultant, and marketing support for an electronic publishing effort. She holds bachelor's degrees in botany and English from University of Illinois in Champaign-Urbana, where she also obtained her M.L.S. at the Graduate School of Library Science.

INTRODUCTION

The term "library network" can be interpreted in a number of ways. What we mean by the term is an organization that serves libraries and librarians and is typically a membership organization, often a nonprofit corporation; and can be thought of as a distributor and/or value-added reseller. Networks were established to promote resource sharing and the use of modern technologies for the benefit of library patrons, and this is still the principal mission of networks.

We realize that this description is not terribly limiting, so we will cite some examples. The organization for which we work, PALINET, is a nonprofit membership corporation. Its members are libraries and information centers situated (for the most part) in Delaware, the District of Columbia, Maryland, New Jersey, and Pennsylvania. PALINET's members span the range of types and sizes of libraries and information centers. (1)

Positions within networks generally fall into one of the following basic categories:

Executive Director & Associate or Assistant Director—overall management and direction
Department Manager—management of specific organizational unit

Coordinator—professional position, subdivided by major specialty, e.g., OCLC services coordinator, microcomputer services coordinator, or similar position

Business Manager—responsible for network financial matters

Clerical positions—e.g., receptionist, secretary, accounts clerk, general clerical, data entry operator

Special positions—information services, editor, marketing, computer operations, accountant, production supervisor, preservation services

Most library networks exhibit similar characteristics: their territories are states or multiple states; their memberships are diverse in size and type, as well as in mission, interests, and resources; they employ small numbers of staff (both professional and clerical) who must be generalists to a considerable degree; and they act as distributors of technology-based products and services to their members. The prices charged are usually competitive and are offered with value-added support and service, which makes these products and services more attractive to members than those obtained through alternative means. (2)

The role of networks is generally to help libraries improve service to their clientele, to foster use of modern technologies for this purpose, and to assist in training library staff to take advantage of technology so as to increase library staff efficiency and to provide an expanding range of information resources to their clientele. Networks frequently enter into alliances with state library agencies and other organizations for the benefit of libraries and their clientele. Networks also serve as advocates of libraries and library service, and from time to time may obtain grants to assist their members in various ways.

There are twenty major library networks in the United States and Canada that fit the above description. These are: AMIGOS, BCR, CAPCON, CLASS, FLICC/FEDLINK,

ILLINET, INCOLSA, MINITEX, MLC, MLNC, NEBASE, NELINET, OHIONET, PACNET, PALINET, PRLC, SOLINET, SUNY/OCLC, UTLAS, and WILS. Figure 1 shows the approximate territory of each of these networks (3), while Table 1 gives their full names and addresses. In addition to these, there are many smaller networks that provide services to libraries in a multicounty area or to a particular class of libraries. Examples of the former include the six regional library systems in New Jersey (4), the District Library Centers in Pennsylvania (5), the Area Library Service Organizations in Ohio (6), the ALSAs in Indiana (7), and the 3Rs Council in New York (8). Examples of the latter include the Health Sciences Libraries Consortium (9) and Triangle Research Libraries Network (10). These smaller networks are often members of the major library networks.

Services and products provided by networks to their members include:

- online reference and full text retrieval services (e.g., OCLC, RLIN, UTLAS, Dialog, BRS, Data Star, VuText, UMI, and EasyNet)

- CD-ROM databases (e.g., SilverPlatter, Wilson, Dialog on Disc, PAIS, and many others)

- database preparation and processing

- consulting (e.g., automation, telecommunication, space planning, bar coding, organization and staffing)

- microcomputers and related equipment (workstations, optical scanners, bar code readers, CD-ROM and other optical storage devices, printers, voice recognition equipment, special equipment for the handicapped, etc.)

- local area networks (including CD-ROM local

area networks)

- software of all kinds

- preservation and conservation services

- telecommunication support (including Internet access)

- electronic mail

- training and continuing education

- management and accounting services

Most such products and services are procured by a network from producers or wholesalers at substantial discounts, and these discounts can be passed on to network members (11).

It is beyond the scope of this chapter to provide more detail on library networks, but the brief introduction above should serve as adequate background for a discussion of the nature of the work performed by network staff.

NATURE OF THE WORK

Work performed by staff of a library network can be organized into five broad categories:

- telephone and on-site support and troubleshooting;

- training and continuing education;

- consulting;

- marketing and sales; and

- administration and management.

Because the ratio of network members to network staff is high (typically twenty members per staff member), network staff generally must perform work in several of these categories.

At PALINET for example, most staff are expected to provide members with capable support and troubleshooting, to conduct workshops and seminars for the benefit of member library staff, to consult with members on a wide variety of matters requiring considerable technical expertise, to market and sell to members the wide variety of products and services the network makes available to them, and to perform accounting and other management and administrative functions.

In a typical day, PALINET staff may answer numerous phone calls for assistance with a variety of problems, such as how to catalog a certain item, how to delete holdings from OCLC's online catalog, how to bar code a collection, or how to get a refund for the unused portion of a service the member wishes to cancel.

Staff may deal with phone calls about how to order equipment, solve problems with a CD-ROM database, retrieve a data file accidentally lost, get a piece of equipment repaired, interpret a bill received from the network. Staff may assist members with the development of a request for proposals, conduct a workshop on interlibrary loan policies, or develop a new workshop on establishing a CD-ROM local area network.

Staff may prepare a mailing to announce a special program or one informing members of a new service or a change in pricing. Staff may work with librarians by phone or in person to define the processing requirements for preparing

MARC records to be loaded into a local automated library system. Network staff may travel to a member library to train library staff in the use of OCLC's EPIC service, or to install a workstation or an entire local area network.

Staff may perform accounting tasks, receive monies and pay bills, prepare invoices for services rendered and products delivered, plan and execute investments, talk with prospective members about the benefits of network membership and the products and services of which they may avail themselves.

Network staff may deal with several different vendors to obtain products needed by members or to solve technical problems related to their products or services. Staff may negotiate agreements with vendors as well as members, and may deal with attorneys, both for members and for vendors.

Staff may participate in meetings, exhibit network services and products at a state library association meeting, or perform on-site consulting for a member on space planning.

In short, on a typical day network staff will perform a variety of tasks that require a wide range of skills, broad knowledge, experience in the library/information industry. Most network staff would, probably, deny that there *is* such a thing as a typical day.

Although it is true that individual network staff have certain principal specialties as their primary responsibility, networks cannot afford the degree of specialization staff exhibit in most libraries. Again, using PALINET as an example, one staff member might have as a major specialization interlibrary loan and reference services (e.g., online databases, CD-ROM), but would also handle matters related to Internet, and telecommunication software (e.g., Procomm Plus), and would conduct workshops in Lotus 1-2-3^R. Another staff member might specialize in microcomputer software such as dBase IV[R] and PageMaker[R], but would also be responsible for hardware installations in member libraries, conducting workshops in local area networking and microcomputer troubleshooting and maintenance.

Still another staff member might handle orders for CD-ROM database products, conduct workshops on Q&A[R] and on an introduction to the MacIntosh computer, and provide support for the network's electronic mail system. Yet another staff member might have the network's publications as a major responsibility, but in addition would handle arrangements for all workshops and seminars, plan and schedule exhibits, prepare minutes of board and other committee meetings, and obtain information for other staff members.

Management in most networks is strictly working management. For example, a staff member might be principally responsible for managing several other staff members (including personnel management, organizing and monitoring the work of the staff, solving problems, conducting meetings, working with other managers, and the like), but would also execute OCLC profile change requests for member libraries, conduct workshops on authority control, write papers (this one, for example), and speak to students of a library school about careers in networks.

Other managers, including the executive director, might be responsible for administration of the network's finances and the accounts of its members, attend board meetings and deal with board members, interact with counterparts in other networks, and maintain the benefits program of the network. Still other managers may prepare responses to requests for proposals, seek outside funding for special projects, conduct workshops on telecommunication, deliver and install equipment in member libraries, prepare financial statements and projections, summarize sales, develop and maintain operating policies and procedures, and write special-purpose software to meet particular member or staff needs.

Network staff and management also participate in professional organizations, write papers, and give presentations of a professional nature, whose subject matter is often not directly related to their work assignments.

In most networks, the nature of the work that staff must perform is varied, changes continually, and demands a great deal of knowledge, experience, flexibility, energy, and dedication.

QUALIFICATIONS

Network careers require staff with qualifications that are, to say the least, uncommon in the librarianship profession. (12) The qualifications of individual staff members vary according to the nature of their respective assignments, but there are certain qualities that most network staff have in common. All must show uncommon dedication, be capable of working with a great variety of people (roles, temperaments, education, experience, age, origins), have and continue to develop knowledge of a wide variety about information products and services, be committed to and have experience with technology, learn quickly and routinely, exhibit mental agility, be capable of delivering instruction to audiences of all sizes, have pleasant and energetic personalities, and be largely self-motivated and self-directed.

Not every member of a network staff needs to have a library degree, but a strong knowledge of library and information center operations and services is important. Also, virtually every member of a network staff must have basic computer skills, in order to use the wide variety of products and services that the network employs in its own operations and provides to its members. The ability to write computer programs is also desirable, and at least one member of the network staff should have this ability. Few schools of library and information science provide the background and training needed for a career in a network. (13)

Most network staff will need to have actual experience gained from working in a library or information center, or from working with information providers. Network staff need to know how to teach, to be able to speak before audiences of various sizes, to write well, and to communicate effectively by telephone.

Network staff should have both a library/information science specialty (e.g., cataloging, online searching, public service, preservation/conservation, administration) and a subject specialty (e.g., chemistry, music, art, engineering, history, psychology, business). Although the ability to speak a foreign language is not essential, it is often very beneficial and desirable.

Some networks employ staff with specialties in marketing and sales, although in most networks, these functions are performed by staff with other primary duties.

In addition, network staff generally should enjoy travel and be capable of dealing with all sorts of unexpected events. And above all else they must have an unquenchable desire to learn and to impart their knowledge to staff of member libraries and others.

Those staff who aspire to management roles within a network must also have management experience. Although an M.B.A. is not necessary, those who have earned such a degree would be considered better qualified to manage (recognizing that networks are nonprofit organizations, whereas M.B.A. programs focus on the for profit sector).

For all network staff positions (listed earlier), the qualifications we have described above are applicable. Of course, certain positions also call for specialized knowledge and skills that may not be applicable to others.

PROS AND CONS

Having pointed out that networks are unusual organizations, and that the qualifications of staff must be extraordinary, it is fair to consider the benefits and disadvantages of a career in a library network.

Perhaps the greatest advantage of working in a network environment is that there is never a dull moment. Network jobs are demanding both of intellect and energy, but it is these very qualities that keep you on the leading edge of the library and information service industry and continuously invigorated.

It is, however, often the case that a person cannot sustain the required pace over many years and so may seek alternative employment. This condition is often referred to as "burnout," because the person has performed at a high level of effort for so long that he or she can no longer sustain such effort. Relatively few people who seek careers in library networks retire from those careers.

Because network staffs are generally small, the opportunity for advancement is limited, although the number of networks makes cross-organizational advancement possible. Perhaps more important than advancement is the opportunity to directly influence the evolution of library and information service. A real sense of accomplishment is often more important that a job title.

Salaries are generally higher for positions in library networks than for comparable positions in libraries and information centers. (14) In a sense however, this fact can also be a disadvantage, since higher salaries tend to make it difficult to move from a network position back into a library.

Instead, network staff generally move to other corporate environments, such as automation vendors, database producers, corporate information centers, and their own consulting businesses.

In summary, a career in library networks is quite rewarding, and provides one of the best learning experiences a librarian can have. Moreover, the knowledge and experience gained will stand you in good stead in many related enterprises if a long-term network career is not what you choose to pursue.

REFERENCES

1. PALINET. *Annual Report 1990/91*. Philadelphia, PA: PALINET; 1991 [published only in machine-readable form].

2. (a) Stevens, N.; Rush, J. E. *Issues relative to the role of state and multi-state networks in the evolving nationwide bibliographic network*. Powell, OH: James E. Rush Associates; 1981: p. 8–12.
   (b) Markuson, B. E.; Woolls, B. (eds.) *Networks for networkers: critical issues in cooperative library development*. New York, NY: Neal-Schuman Publishers; 1979. 444p.
   (c) OCLC Online Computer Library Center. *OCLC at a glance: OCLC Services for Libraries*. Dublin, OH: The Center; 1991. p. 12–13.

3. (a) Stevens, N.; Rush, J. E. Appendix B.
   (b) OCLC Online Computer Library Center. *Introducing OCLC*. Dublin, OH: The Center; 1991. p. 12–13.

4. Studdiford, A. (ed.) *Official Directory of New Jersey Libraries and Media Centers: Including Funding, 1990*. Bayside, NY: LDA; 1990: p. xx, 1.

5. *Directory: Pennsylvania Libraries 1990.* (Prepared by the Library Development Division of the State Library of Pennsylvania.) Harrisburg, PA: State Library of Pennsylvania; 1990. p. 5–6.

6. *American Library Directory, 1991–92.* 44th ed. New York: R. R. Bowker; 1991. p. 2256.

7. *Ibid.*, p. 2253.

8. *Ibid.*, p. 2255.

9. Flowers, J.L. Triangle Research Libraries Network: planning for automating the acquisition/serials control function. *Acquisitions Librarian.* (1): 17–31; 1989.

10. Simon, A. C. Development and implementation of a microcomputer-based multi-user MEDLINE system. *Medical Reference Services Quarterly.* 10(2): 1–9; 1991.

11. PALINET. *Service programs: an overview.* Philadelphia, PA: PALINET; 1992. 20p. Document no. PA008.

12. Melin, N. J. Professional without portfolio. The network librarian. *Wilson Library Bulletin.* 54(5): 308–310; 1980.

13. International Federation of Library Associations. Library Schools and Other Training Aspects Section. Education and Research Division. *Papers.* (Presented at the 48th Annual Meeting, Montreal, Canada, August 22–28, 1982.) Washington, DC: EDRS; 1992. (ED227 873)

14. *Survey of salaries and benefits provided by regional networks.* Available from the Regional OCLC Network Directors Advisory Committee (RONDAC) office at OCLC, 6565 Frantz Road, Dublin, OH 43017-3395.

ADDITIONAL REFERENCES

Besemer, S. P. Criteria for the evaluation of library networks. *Resource Sharing and Information Networks*. 4(1): 17–38; 1987.

Kruger, B. NELINET: a case study of regional library network development. *Information Technology and Libraries*. 4(2): 112–121; 1985.

Martin, S. K. Balancing needs: the ideal network of the future. *Journal of Library Automation*. 8(3/4): 131–141; 1987.

Sellen, B. C.; Berkner, D. S. (eds.) *New options for librarians: finding a job in a related field*. New York: Neal-Schuman Publishers; 1984. 313p.

Figure 1. Approximate geographical territories of the twenty largest library networks.

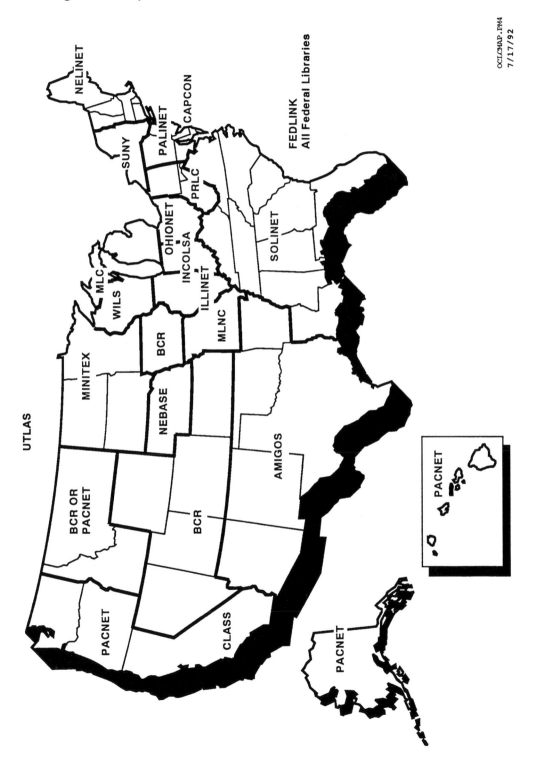

Table 1. Names and addresses of the twenty largest library networks.

AMIGOS Bibliographic Council, Inc.
12200 Park Central Drive
Suite 500
Dallas, TX 75251

BCR Bibliographical Center for Research
4500 Cherry Creek Drive South
Suite 206
Denver, CO 80222

CAPCON
1320 19th Street N.W.
Suite 400
Washington, DC 20036

CLASS (Cooperative Library Agency for Systems and Services)
1415 Koll Circle
Suite 101
San Jose, CA 95112-4698

FLICC/FEDLINK (Federal Library and Information Center Committee)
Library of Congress
Washington, DC 20540

ILLINET (ILLINET/OCLC Services)
Illinois State Library
300 South Second Street
Springfield, IL 62701-1796

INCOLSA (Indiana Cooperative Library Services Authority)
5929 Lakeside Boulevard
Indianapolis, IN 46278-1966

MINITEX (MINITEX Library Information Network)
S-33 Wilson Library
University of Minnesota
309 19th Avenue South
Minneapolis, MN 55455-0414

MLC (Michigan Library Consortium)
6810 Cedar Street
Suite 8
Lansing, MI 48911

MLNC (Missouri Library Network Corporation)
10332 Old Olive Street Road
St. Louis, MO 63141

NEBASE (Nebraska Library Commission)
1420 P Street
Lincoln, NE 68508-1683

NELINET (NELINET Inc.)
Two Newton Executive Park
Newton, MA 02162

OCLC/PACNET (OCLC Pacific Network)
9227 Haven Avenue
Suite 260
Rancho Cucamonga, CA 91730

OHIONET
1500 West Lane Avenue
Columbus, OH 43221-3975

PALINET
3401 Market Street
Suite 262
Philadelphia, PA 19104

PRLC
103 Yost Boulevard
Pittsburgh, PA 15221

SOLINET (Southeastern Library Network, Inc.)
1438 Pearchtree Street N.W.
Atlanta, GA 30309-2955

SUNY/OCLC
State University of New York
State University Plaza
Albany, NY 12246

Utlas International Canada
3300 Bloor Street West
West Tower, 16th Floor
Etobicoke, Ontario
Canada M8X 2X2

WILS (Wisconsin Interlibrary Services)
728 State Street
Room 464
Madison, WI 53706

TED SLATE
DIRECTOR OF RESEARCH SERVICES FOR A NEWSMAGAZINE

Ted Slate is director of research services for *Newsweek*, 444 Madison Ave., New York, NY 10022. He has held this position since April 1990. He began his library career at the Library of Congress, then moved to the Washington office of *The New York Times*, where he served as librarian. Later he returned to the Arms Control and Disarmament Bibliography section at the Library of Congress. In 1966 he became library director at *Newsweek*. Beginning in 1988 Mr. Slate was promoted to a series of positions, leading to his present title. He received a B.A. from Rutgers University, followed by two master's degrees from the University of Michigan, in history and library science. He received the distinguished alumnus award from Michigan in 1988. Active in many library-oriented organizations, including the Special Libraries Association, Mr. Slate has served on several major boards, including the New York State Commissioner of Education's Committee on Statewide Library Development.

INTRODUCTION

It's comforting to think that we play the major role in shaping "the grand design" of our lives. But as it pertains to my career choices made over the years, nothing has been further from the truth.

From the time I completed my library education, every job change--and there were a number of them in the early years—occurred when I found myself working at something I was perfectly happy with and suddenly a phone would ring or I was called into someone's office and asked if I would be interested in a new challenge.

I received one such call in late 1965, while employed at the Library of Congress. A *Newsweek* editor was on the phone asking if I wanted to be considered for the recently vacated position of library director. Having previously worked at the *New York Times*, and finding myself missing the news business terribly, I jumped at the opportunity and joined *Newsweek* in January 1966.

From the start, I thoroughly enjoyed my position as *Newsweek*'s Library Director, and I remember thinking in the early years that my job-hopping days were finally over. In the twenty three years that I held that position I came to look forward to retiring from it eventually. But there was no way to anticipate that a faltering economy would affect that plan as well.

In the fall of 1988, in anticipation of uncertain economic times ahead, *Newsweek* offered early-retirement incentives to a large number of its long-term employees; many accepted the offer and left at year end. One department adversely affected by this transition was the Letters department, whose entire management team accepted the offer and departed within a three-month period.

Shortly thereafter--and it came as a complete surprise to me--the editor asked me to take over the letters department, reorganize it so that it operated with a reduced staff, and manage it *and* the Library.

I now began splitting my time between the letters department and the library and, by early 1990, the reorganization was completed. During this fifteen-month restructuring, in addition to managing the library, I conducted research for the news staff (I loathed giving up some of the hands-on work that I loved to do); selected and edited letters for publication in the "Letters" column; designed and supervised the installation of a PC-based, local area network to replace the letters department's antiquated IBM 5520 system for letter preparation--and performed a multitude of other tasks too numerous to list.

This was an extremely difficult period--long hours at the office often stretching into the evening and with more than the occasional weekend of work. Fifteen months without a real vacation had begun to get to me. I had to tell the editor, and soon, that I needed additional help--and a break.

However, before I could get to him, he called me to his office to say that the chief of research was leaving and he wanted me to add the research department to my present responsibilities—and I should include the copy desk and the proofreading departments as well. He said that while I would still have responsibility for the library and the letters areas, I would have to relinquish my library director and letters editor positions and appoint new heads of those departments, create a new designation for myself, and hire whatever assistance I needed to run the five departments.

The job was a newly created position, director of research services, administering those departments responsible for the factual accuracy of the magazine. Without a minute's hesitation, I accepted the job and left for vacation.

NATURE OF THE WORK

My present position offers what few others do--the opportunity to be involved at every stage with the launching of a product; in this case, a weekly magazine. The week begins on Tuesday, when I attend the weekly story conference. Here the editors sketch out the stories being planned for their departments (e.g., national affairs, arts, business, etc.), and I get the first indication of my staffing requirements for the coming week. During the week, the researchers, reporters, and librarians on my staff interview sources and glean information from printed materials--information which will form the basis for stories to be written or used to verify material being gathered elsewhere.

The week ends on Saturday when others of my staff check facts, copyedit, and proofread the finished stories before transmitting them to those who print and distribute the magazine.

Normally, and unless there are legal problems with a written piece, my direct association with any given issue ends three weeks after its appearance on the newsstands. In the weeks after publication, the letters department receives letters from readers--some twelve hundred or more weekly--informing the magazine how pleased or unhappy they are with our product. If we've screwed up--or if they think we have--some twenty million readers are out there to tell us. Each of these letters receives a reply--and a representative selection of them appear in the magazine's "Letters" column. Each week, I review and edit the column before sending it on to the editor for final approval.

For a letter that threatens legal action or when the letter writer is particularly aggrieved, the point of contention is carefully reresearched and, if there appears to be a basis for the complaint, the letter is discussed with the legal staff. It then remains for my office to resolve the matter quickly and directly with the letter writer and to put it behind us before lawyers begin talking to lawyers and the issue takes on a life of its own.

QUALIFICATIONS

In my present position, I deal with editorial staffers in all departments and at every level. The creative process in journalism is one I've marveled at for twenty eight years, and I now have the opportunity to view and be a part of it from a different vantage point, up close and from start to finish.

Over the years, I've rarely spent time thinking about my career at *Newsweek*--frankly, I've been too busy. But, since leaving the field of librarianship and then being asked to prepare this chapter, I've given the matter a good deal of thought, particularly dwelling on what I did as library director that might have influenced the editors to believe that I was capable of handling other duties as well. Let me share some of these thoughts with you.

First, I made it a condition of my employment that I attend those meetings where decisions were reached regarding our editorial product. In addition to the obvious value of these meetings—that decisions here affected on the library's work—they also brought me in constant contact with the top editors who, consciously or not, were sizing up my ability to function as a manager.

I always believed that what my management thought of me personally and professionally determined in large measure the extent to which they were willing to commit a substantial portion of the company's resources to my charge. This said, it's not surprising then that announcements of the SLA and other offices I've held over the years, or speeches I've given, found their way into the company's newsletter.

Second, I never subscribed to the maxim that dedicated and quality library service was always rewarded. Since most of the effort of the library was normally directed toward 95% or more of the *Newsweek* staff having little or no say over the library's budget, I always found it necessary to fashion alternative methods to reach those who ultimately made budgetary decisions.

Third, in addition to carrying out the library's primary

mission—to provide informational support to *Newsweek's* researchers, writers, and editors—I always found the resources to offer library services to *Newsweek's* business departments, particularly our two main revenue streams, the circulation and advertising departments. While this effort represented a fraction of our total reference services, the library, and I, benefitted disproportionately to the volume of this activity.

Fourth, I always tried to incorporate into the library unsupervised activities located in other areas of the company, and to keep tabs on functions that previously had been scattered among many other departments. Whenever a new opportunity involving organization and record keeping presented itself—and where it related, even tangentially, to the library's raison d'être—I offered the library's expertise in managing these functions. The maintenance of the Editorial Comp List, coordination of all microform activities within the company, whether it involved dealing with the vendors who sell microform editions of *Newsweek* or providing services such as microfilming of canceled securities of The Washington Post Company—these were just a few of the responsibilities the library assumed over the years. Once again, while these efforts didn't represent the substance of what the library did on a day-to-day basis, they were responsibilities that brought me, on a regular basis, in close contact with my management.

Fifth, my communications to management about what the library was accomplishing rarely conveyed in traditional units of library measurement, such as materials acquired and circulated, bibliographies prepared, etc. They were almost always couched in measurements that reflected impact, particularly on those profit sectors which our corporate officers closely and continually monitored. I always felt that what *Newsweek's* management wanted to hear from me was the part the library played in getting that account, how we assisted in selling that ad, and how we backed up that sales presentation.

Sixth, and perhaps most important of all, is LUCK—being the right person in the right place at the right time. Over the years I've known some very able librarians who, through corporate reorganizations, had the misfortune of finding themselves reporting to a financial officer or a manager of company services, neither of which was interested in libraries. For me, LUCK won out every time.

In summary, what I've tried to point out here is that it wasn't necessary to leave the library to expand my influence beyond it, and to earn sufficient regard for my work so that the editor would consider me for other, higher-level positions.

PROS AND CONS

It would be misleading to suggest that the work is completely exhilarating and satisfying. As with almost every activity, there are advantages and disadvantages and here are a few of them.

On the plus side, I have been given the opportunity to shape *Newsweek*'s research efforts for years to come. There are similarities among the departments that report to me and I now have the opportunity, without going through a lot of red tape--i.e., having to check with other department heads--to restructure parts of my operation, shift functions from one department to another if it is more logical for the other department to perform them, or, at the very least, to be able to temporarily transfer personnel from one department to another to relieve temporary crises.

Another advantage is that things get done more quickly now. My previous work as library director often brought me in close contact with all of the departments I now administer, but if I wanted another department to carry on where the library left off, it wasn't always possible to persuade the other department head to do it. Now all I have to do is persuade myself that something is necessary, speak to the appropriate department head, and the job gets done. On many matters, therefore, it's no longer necessary to consult management because, in those instances, I am management!

On the downside, much of my work in the library and, later, the letters department, dealt with substantive matters. In the library, especially, more often than not I worked on research projects that allowed me to delve deeply into a wide variety of subjects. Now, there are days--not many, but enough of them--when I leave the office wondering what exactly I have accomplished other than having put out half a dozen fires around the company. I sometimes get the feeling that my knowledge base has been reconfigured to measure a quarter inch deep and ten miles wide.

And I miss the give-and-take of mixing it up with my staff and bouncing ideas off of them on a wide variety of matters--e.g., working out the nitty-gritty problems of where to find additional shelving space, deciding how to attack that large research problem and then doing it, etc.

With the freedom and authority associated with my present level of management comes more exposure, responsibility and vulnerability--and that can be more than a little disconcerting. On balance, however, and lest you think I harbor regrets about having assumed my new job, the step I took is one I wouldn't want to reverse.

It should come as no surprise, based on what I said earlier, that on some occasions the frustrations of my new job seem overwhelming, and I get to wondering how long I'll keep it up before I call it quits. Inevitably, whenever this happens, I think about Phil, a guy who worked for the circus for twenty five years in a job that required him to get up every day at sunrise, put on a pair of boots, grab a shovel, and spend the day cleaning out the cages of the large mammals. After one particularly grueling day, he returned home, showered, and mustered whatever remaining strength he had to pull himself to the dining room table. Across from him, his wife pleaded, "Phil, give it up. Every year, for twenty five years, you've shoveled out those cages. Look at you. Enough's enough!" Phil looked up at her in disbelief and replied, "What? And give up show business?"

Show biz—in this case, the news biz—has had an overwhelming appeal for me as well, and I expect to rise each morning, grab my shovel, and tackle the job for some years to come.

MEGAN SNIFFIN-MARINOFF
ARCHIVIST/CURATOR AT A COLLEGE LIBRARY

Megan Sniffin-Marinoff is college archivist/curator of special collections and director of the archives management program, Simmons College Graduate School of Library and Information Science, 300 The Fenway, Boston, MA 02115. After college Ms. Sniffin-Marinoff worked for a few years in public relations and journalism positions before returning to college for graduate work, upon completion of which she accepted her present position. She has a B.A. in journalism from Boston University and an M.A. in history and a Certificate in Archives Management, Historical Editing, and the Administration of Historical Societies from New York University. Ms. Sniffin-Marinoff has served as a consultant to numerous universities and organizations. She has been active in The New England Archivists (currently serving as president) and other archival and historical professional societies.

INTRODUCTION

As I suspect is the case with most people in my profession, I stumbled upon a career in archives. Despite the fact that I had some knowledge about archives from newspaper-related research projects and through personal, genealogical investigations, it never occurred to me that archivists had interesting jobs or were part of a profession with specialized training and traditions.

After working for a few years after college in public relations and journalism positions, I realized it was the research aspect of newspaper work that most interested me. Deciding to strengthen my research skills and historical background, I entered a master's program in history at New York University. At that time the university was in the early years of a joint program in history and archival management, historical editing, and the administration of historical societies. Since the editing portion of the program seemed to complement my earlier training and piqued my interest, I decided to attend both programs.

An appointment as a graduate assistant in the University Archives thrust me immediately into the throes of archival work. One of my first jobs was to assist in organizing the papers of a former president of the university whose topics of correspondence ranged from the growing diversity of ethnic backgrounds of New Yorkers and the resulting change in the NYU student population, to his personal letters written home in the aftermath of the San Francisco earthquake of 1906. I was hooked. To this day I cannot believe that people actually pay me to do work that I find intellectually stimulating, exciting, and fulfilling and once sent me halfway around the world.

NATURE OF THE WORK

In the words of University of Texas Professor David Gracy, archives are "the records, organically related, of an entity, systematically maintained (normally after they have fulfilled the purpose for which they were created), because they contain information of continuing value." (1) Collections of such records are the deliberately maintained documents of organizations, institutions, families, and individuals. As record keeping practices have changed, so too have the types of records archivists collect. "Traditional" paper-based, textual records such as files, ledgers, diaries, or engineering drawings as well as photographs, film, sound recordings, videotape, and electronic records are but a few of the formats familiar to today's archivist. (2)

Unlike the allied "cousins" in the cultural arena, libraries and museums, archives are little understood. With archives often perceived as dead storage or an accumulation of unwanted, dusty files or old, useless data, the profession has had to battle an image problem. In fact, dust and useless files are anathema to modern archives. With the weight of the accumulation of decaying records on their shoulders, those managing successful archival programs have had to modernize; take preservation seriously; justify a program's existence; and provide a useful function to a parent organization, individuals, or society-at-large. As stated in a brochure distributed by the Society of American Archivists (SAA), the profession's natural association of individuals and institutions interested in the preservation and use of records, archives have been used successfully to "Protect your rights...Increase profits...Trace your genealogy...Preserve historic buildings...Sustain historical research...Provide administrative continuity...Educate and entertain." (3)

Generally speaking, archivists manage institutional or organizational records and personal papers. Archives management consists of several basic functions: appraisal, or working with others to determine which records to retain; acquisition, or the physical work and paperwork required to obtain and add records to a collection; arrangement and description, or ordering materials and creating the tools to enable their use; preservation, or housing and handling records in accordance with accepted standards and working with professional conservators to solve problems; and providing access and reference service, or activities ranging from deciding who can use records to offering directions for use to making a collection's holdings widely known.

The term **archives** refers not only to actual records, but also to the places or agencies where archives are kept. Archivists thus find work in a variety of sites. Some archivists work for public agencies whose purpose is to document the activities of government at every level. Such agencies include the U. S. National Archives (NARA) located in Washington, D.C., as well as in the many presidential libraries and federal record centers across the country, state archives, and various city or municipal archives. Archival collections are also maintained by many private institutions or organizations, for profit and not-for-profit, and, as such, archival positions can be obtained in a wide range of settings, including cultural organizations (museums, symphonies, dance companies), colleges and universities, labor unions, religious organizations, philanthropic foundations, businesses, scientific organizations, hospitals, etc.

Institutional, organizational, and personal papers also are often maintained outside the creating agency or home and are deposited in manuscript repositories, historical societies, and libraries whose main purpose is to collect historical materials. Archivists who work in these settings, in some cases with the title of curator or manuscript librarian, can work alongside general administrators, librarians, museum curators, documentary editors, and educators interested in the same subject.

While my current joint appointment as both archivist and professor of archival education is unique, it is indicative of the variety of circumstances in which an archivist can find him or herself. Archival work, in most cases, requires full-time-attention. Our staff of one and a half full-time equivalent professionals, students, and with some technical assistance from the college library staff, maintains a full-time archival operation. The department provides the almost one hundred year old undergraduate college, numerous graduate programs, and four graduate schools, not only with a traditional institutional archives, but also support for growing manuscript and rare book collections.

In a single week staff might answer numerous reference questions, from both in-house and outside scholars; correspond with prospective donors about their personal papers; visit offices to answer questions about office files; and meet briefly with visiting alumni. All the while, the staff continues to process various collections with activities ranging from opening new boxes; rehousing and analyzing materials; creating guides to contents; and writing MARC records for the holdings in order to link up with college and national databases. Other week's activities might include meeting with college administrators to discuss records transfers; planning or executing exhibits; conducting an oral history with a former college official or faculty member; assisting development officers with background information on prospective donors; speaking to groups of students, faculty, and staff about anything ranging from college traditions to architectural history; planning preservation activity for either restoration or microfilm; researching and planning for technological improvements; or even leading "trolley tours" for students and alumni through the city with a Simmons College history theme. Each day is different, and the work is never dull.

Exploring avenues for occasional professional revitalization or simply as an extension of archival duties or responsibilities is common in the field. My additional interests brought me to teaching. Some archivists, quite involved in their areas of subject expertise, become authors. Others, particularly those who work in institutional or organizational archives, often become so knowledgeable about the day-to-day workings of their parent company they take on additional work in related departments, such as records management centers, or move into completely new positions in other departments such as development, public relations, or even the upper reaches of management.

Many archivists also moonlight as consultants. More often than not this activity occurs as happenstance and after years of experience. Some archivists eventually choose the consultant's life and either set up shop on their own or join an established firm. (4) Consulting work can add an interesting dimension and depth to your professional career. My own experiences have afforded me the opportunity to advise on the development of archives in educational institutions and a bank, to plan three major exhibits, and to plan for the collection and move of the records of a major medical and educational project in West Africa.

QUALIFICATIONS

Generally speaking, to obtain an entry-level position in today's job market, employers who understand the field require some kind of graduate level coursework, more often than not leading to degrees either in library science or history and including classes in various aspects of archives management. While in the past many archives were run by those who received postappointment training, today's established archives often require prospective employees not only to have preappointment, in-class training, but also some hands-on experience, usually obtained in internships. A 1992 survey of job requirements posted between 1988 and 1992 in the employment listings of the *SAA Newsletter* and the *SAA Employment Bulletin* completed for Simmons College shows that in 1991 employers requested the following: M.L.S. (13.95 percent), M.A./ history (5.82 percent), M.L.S. or M.A. (48.84 percent), M.L.S. and M.A. (22.09 percent), Ph.D. (3.49 percent), and other degrees (5.81 percent). Nearly every advertisement requested some form of graduate-level, archival coursework, and 54.56 percent required technical competency. (5)

The major exception to the requirement for extensive preappointment archival coursework is, surprisingly, the U.S. National Archives. For a variety of reasons, including the fact that NARA runs an elaborate in-house training program, a graduate degree in political science or history will prove more beneficial, at present, for employment opportunities there.

Also, employers from institutions establishing new archival programs often do not know that archivists are part of a distinct profession and understandably might engage well-intentioned but poorly equipped people. Without an understanding of the dimensions of archival work, employers hire those ranging from file clerks to retired chairmen of the board. Quite often it is this group that comprises the majority of those seeking postappointment training in graduate schools, institutes, and workshops.

While the profession hopes to guide employers to more intelligent and considered hiring practices by better publicity of the profession's existence and the publication of literature or brochures such as that of the Archivists Round Table of Metropolitan New York and the Mid-Atlantic Regional Archives Conference's *Selecting an Archivist* (1985), it is impossible to distribute this literature to the great unknown. Archival consultants, often brought in to assist institutions establish an archival program, can guide the hiring practices of prospective archives employers, but such consultants are not associated with the opening of every new archives. Since the archival profession in this country is relatively young, the opening of new archives is fertile ground for the growth of the profession and future employment opportunities. (6) While the opening of new archives is good news for the profession, it does mean the postappointment versus preappointment training dilemma will continue for some time.

The question of how you prepare for a career in archives is one of the most contentious issues facing the archival profession today. A great deal has been written about the short history of archival education in the United States, particularly concerning the benefits and drawbacks of pre- and postappointment training and history versus library science-based programs. (7) The latest controversy involves the U.S. adaptation of a model for educational programs in use in Canada that takes graduate archival education beyond the SAA-recommended minimum three-course sequence to a full master's degree in archives administration. U.S. archivists have yet to cast their vote on this new program development. Unlike the American Library Association, which accredits schools of library and information science, the Society of

American Archivists instead offers a set of guidelines for graduate level archival education. The SAA periodically publishes a directory to archival education programs in the United States and Canada. The directory describes the variety of graduate and undergraduate, single-and multi course programs, institutes, and regularly scheduled continuing education workshops offered in colleges, universities, and other organizations in the United State and Canada. (8)

For those choosing the institute or workshop route, many regional associations, such as the New England Archivists or the Midwest Archives Conference, offer noncredit workshops and seminars. Particularly for those working in small, part-time organizations seeking postappointment training, the workshop route has been popular. (9)

While educational qualifications for archival employment are important, those seeking to enter and succeed in the archival profession need special personal qualities, too. Unfortunately, the steadfast stereotypes of archives as dusty, musty, mysterious, and dank basements and archivists as quiet, odd, eccentric characters endure as much as the various stereotypes of such other professionals as librarians, teachers, accountants and scientists.

While a certain amount of mystery has its place, and in fact may be part of the allure of the profession for some, the retiring personality usually is not happy with this professional choice. Archives are often active, busy places and especially in the case of one-or two-person operations, can sometimes seem like three-ring circuses. Aside from a love of history or a special subject or area of study, you must like people and papers, order and chaos, solitude and public speaking, the visual and the written, and pencils and computers. As the world progresses, so too does the nature of historical record; an archivist must handle change well.

PROS AND CONS

The main disadvantage to working in the archival profession is the weariness you can experience explaining and even justifying to others what you do and why you do it. If there is ever any accounting of burnout in the profession, this may prove to be a leading factor. The misunderstanding or lack of understanding of what archives are and what archivists do can lead to general frustrations of setting a career path or increasing a salary over time: but in this respect archivists fare no differently from those in the allied library and information professions, at cultural or not-for-profit organizations and institutions, or on the public payroll.

The most satisfying aspect of archival work is the variety of opportunities to learn and grow, personally and professionally. Appraisal and reference activities require archivists to remain on the cutting edge of research trends and allow for development of subject expertise. Organizational activities allow archivists to develop sophisticated technical and managerial competencies. Whether a professional is working in the public or private sphere, the arts or the sciences, with the seventeenth or the twentieth centuries, broadsides or electronic records, there is a place to develop interests and to feel the personal satisfaction of playing a role in an institution's growth and development or the documentation of a subject's history. The fact is, most archivists like to get up in the morning and go to work.

REFERENCES

1. Gracy, David B., II. Archivists, you are what people think you keep. *American Archivist.* 52:76; 1989 Winter.

2. To learn more about the archival profession in general, see the overviews in publications such as:
   a. *ALA World Encyclopedia*, 1986 ed., s.v. "Archives"

b. Bradsher, James Gregory, ed. *Managing archives and archival institutions.* Chicago: University of Chicago Press; 1988.

c. Duckett, Kenneth W. *Modern manuscripts: a practical manual for their management, care, and use.* Nashville: American Association for State and Local History; 1975.

d. O'Toole, James M. *Understanding archives and manuscripts.* Chicago: Society of American Archivists; 1990.

e. Pederson, Ann. *Keeping archives.* Sydney: Australian Society of Archivists; 1987.

3. Society of American Archivists Task Force on Archives and Society. *Who is the "I" in archives?* Chicago: Society of American Archivists; 1986.

4. For information on the backgrounds and specialties of individual archival consultants and firms, see: Society of American Archivists. *1992 Directory of consultants.* Chicago: Society of American Archivists; 1992.

5. Porter, Susan; Sniffin-Marinoff, Megan. *Proposal for a joint degree program in archives management leading to a Master of Science in Library Science and a Master of Arts in History.* Simmons College. 1992 March.

6. Even though historical societies have been in existence in this country since the founding of the Massachusetts Historical Society in 1791 and curators and librarians across the country have been saving records of our nation's history ever since, it was not until the National Archives in 1934 and the establishment of the Society of American Archivists in 1936 that the movement towards a distinct U.S. profession began in earnest.

7. In particular, see:

a. Cox, Richard J. Professionalism and archivists in the United States. *American Archivist.* 49:229–247; 1986

Summer.

    b. Evans, Frank B. The organization and status of archival training: an historical perspective. *Archivum.* 34:75–91; 1988.

    c. Evans, Frank B. Postappointment archival training: a proposed solution for a basic problem. *American Archivist.* 40:57–74; 1977 Jan.

    d. *American Archivist.* 1988 Summer.

    8. The latest edition is: Society of American Archivists, Office of Education. *Education Directory* 1990–1991. Chicago: Society of American Archivists; 1991.

    The SAA's Guidelines for Graduate Archival Education Programs issued in the *American Archivist* 51: 390–398; 1988 Summer are reprinted in the directory.

    9. For a discussion of the issues regarding instruction by regional associations, see: Ericson, Timothy I. Professional associations and archival education: a different role, or a different theater? *American Archivist.* 51:298-341; 1988 Summer.

DAVID WEISBROD
SYSTEMS OFFICER IN A UNIVERSITY LIBRARY

Until recently David Weisbrod was assistant professor,
School of Library Service at Columbia University. He is
currently completing work on his doctoral degree at Rutgers
University's School of Communication, Information and
Library Studies. He was also on the part-time faculty of
Rutgers from 1987 to 1990. Prior to that he was head of the
systems office at Yale University Library (1976–1987) after
holding other jobs at that library from 1964 to 1976. In the
period 1959–1964 he was a programmer for System
Development Corporation. Mr. Weisbrod has an A.B. in
physics from Harvard University and an M.S. in system
analysis from Rutgers University. He has served as a
consultant for various groups; in addition he has written
several papers and reports. Active in several professional
organizations, he has also served as a consultant for a number
of organizations.

INTRODUCTION

I got into systems work through my experience with
the underlying technology--a stereotyped route, but by no
means the only one. Having discovered computers (Univac I)
and programming (in assembly language) in my senior year
in college, and being anxious to divorce myself from an ill-
conceived undergraduate marriage to physics, I started out as
a programmer trainee with System Development Corporation
in Paramus, New Jersey. A variety of assignments, including
lead programmer, technical editor of documentation, and
programming instructor, awakened in me an appreciation for
the broader view of things -- that individual program
modules, no matter how elegantly coded, were only as

valuable as their fit in the operational context; and that the effectiveness of an entire computer application, no matter how beautifully conceived and implemented as technical artifacts, could be determined only in the broader evaluative context of the complete human-machine system (as we called it in the 1950s and 1960s) or of the complete sociotechnical system (in updated 1990s parlance, reflecting a somewhat modified perspective). Thus, the birth and early nurturing of a "systems person."

The so-called typical large university library that supplies the context of the following discussion would be, for example, the library of a reasonably substantial research university, i.e., a library probably satisfying the requirements for membership in the Association of Research Libraries.

NATURE OF THE WORK

Mission and Tasks of the Systems Office

The precise details of the mission of the systems office in a large university library will vary among institutions, but in general that mission is to plan for and provide the library's automated information infrastructure. Such planning and execution typically requires resources (human, tangible, financial, other) unavailable in the various operating units of the library. Among the specific tasks that are commonly entailed here are the following.

1.   *Planning:*
Consists of defining broad institutional goals, of strategic planning (long-term approaches) and tactical planning (short-term details).

2.   *Systems management:*
The systems life cycle (SLC) has been explained in numerous monographs, articles, and texts. The following list indicates the broad range of human skills and expertise

entailed in managing the life cycle of an automated information system from start to finish.

>Phase 1. Preliminary investigation: A brief effort to define the scope of the problem at hand and perform a broad assessment of needs.

>Phase 2. Analysis: Establishing complete understanding of the existing system.

>Phase 3. Design: Planning the new system.

>Phase 4. Constructing the new system.

>Phase 5. Implementation: Converting from the existing system to the new one. This entails such tasks as file conversion, installation of the system "in the field," user training, transition to the new system.

>Phase 6. Operation and evaluation: "steady-state" operation of the system maintenance and fine-tuning evaluation and monitoring the continuing operation for evidence of the need to reiterate through the system life cycle (SLC).

3. *Coordination of infrastructure planning:*
Working with other cognizant offices at the university (those responsible for telephone, data communication, academic computing, administrative information services, etc.).

4. *Evaluation of choices in numerous areas:*
Evaluation of available information systems and/or components (hardware, software, databases) and available services; or evaluation of local (in-house)

development and operation, as an alternative to procurement of available systems and services.

5.   *Recommendation*:
Formulation of recommendations for short- and long-term procurement/development strategies.

6.   *Maintaining expertise and awareness:*
Keeping abreast of developments in information provision, interpreting these developments to library staff and administration, assessing the impact of these developments on the evolving mission of the library.

7.   *Keeping alert:*
Recognizing problems and opportunities for the library--especially those shaped by information technology--and factoring them into the continuing process of review and adjustment of the library's mission.

8.   *Proposing and/or taking initiatives:*
The scope of action can involve the university as well as regional or national venues. The substance can involve anything relating directly or indirectly to the mission of the systems office or the library, e.g., technical standards, legislation, cooperative undertakings.

9.   *Dissemination:*
Publication of research findings, important developments, noteworthy experiences, etc.

10.   *Roles of the individual:*
The individual systems officer fills many roles, including the visionary; technological expert and/or employer of technological experts; systems analyst and/or employer of systems analysts; communicator (in various directions within the organization--upward, laterally, and downward), both as a persuader and as an explainer; manager of projects; provider of services (to various units of the library and/or directly to the library's clientele); interpreter/translator between/among

specialists (or organizations) who do not speak each others' language; researcher; entrepreneur.

11. *Additional skills and expertise:*
In addition to the various technical competencies implied by the tasks and roles listed above, expertise and skill in several additional areas of great importance.

The systems officer must understand traditional librarianship and library management, both "hands-on" practical experience and as well-internalized mastery of underlying theory. This is essential to an ability to recognize issues, be alert to implications, and to be well enough grounded so as not to be bound blindly to current practice, technology, and organization.

The systems officer must be a consummate diplomat. This implies an ability to perceive and understand complex organizational and interpersonal relationships; to think with cool detachment about the melding of the technical and the political in devising strategies for persuasion; and to know unerringly when and where to communicate what to whom, as well as when to maintain silence.

The systems officer must listen, speak, and write well. This is a necessary--though not sufficient--prerequisite for the diplomatic competence discussed immediately above.

The systems officer must be able to tolerate uncertainty and incessant change, to keep track of all of the loose ends entailed in a project, and ultimately to tie together all those loose ends into a coherent plan.

QUALIFICATIONS

No single set of qualifications exists that can be the absolute standard for a person to perform the work of a systems officer. Without question all of the following are useful. A solid grounding in the full range of underlying technologies and in information organization and librarianship and an understanding of the importance of service to end users of information systems. In addition, you need to be temperamentally inclined to perform all the roles listed above. How much of this can be obtained through academic training and how much through on-the-job experience cannot be prescribed.

PROS AND CONS

The major reward of working as a systems officer in a large university library is the opportunity to work in the academic context, i.e., with bright, dedicated, and idealistic people--when it's good, it's very good. The major disadvantage is that often resources fall far short of needs and expectations.

Information and information services are undergoing fundamental change. Changing too is the definition of the university library/research library. Old tensions are being rebalanced and new questions explored, including such matters as these:

- Archive of the record of human culture *versus* service provider for a defined clientele;

- Ownership of materials *versus* access to materials (not necessarily owned locally);

- The virtual library *versus* the physical library; and

- The materials of interest for inclusion in the collections of research libraries are themselves becoming increasingly based in high technology, so that the questions of designing and managing the technology of the library's infrastructure now impinge both on the matter of how the library will conduct its own internal business (acquisitions, cataloging, circulation, etc.) and how the library will make available the collections—and the services—it is charged with providing to its end users.

Regardless of how these matters may be resolved, high technology is increasingly employed in libraries, resulting in more demanding requirements for end-user instruction and assistance. An important implication here is that it must be understood from the very start that systems have to be usable by the full spectrum of individuals in the population of end users. The particular orientation of special libraries and special librarians to the provision of service to end users can serve as a much-needed resource in addressing these challenges.

HELEN L. WILBUR
FIELD REPRESENTATIVE FOR A PRODUCER OF COMPUTER PRODUCTS FOR LIBRARIES

Helen L. Wilbur is account executive/electronic systems serials publishing for University Microfilms, Inc., 300 North Zeeb Road, Ann Arbor, MI 48106. As a librarian, she worked at an investment banking firm, an international oil company, and a metals trade association. Ms. Wilbur spent three years as a trainer for an online vendor, moving into direct sales positions with major vendors of electronic information. She is now a salesperson for a leading company producing many products for libraries, ranging from microfilm to full-text CD-ROM image systems. She received a B.A. in English literature from the University of Chicago and an M.S. from Columbia University's School of Library Service.

INTRODUCTION

I never intended to become a salesperson; in fact, it was one of the last things I would have considered. I was so timid about asking relatives to buy Girl Scout Cookies when I was young that I forced my little brother to do it for me. I moved from librarianship to selling by accident.

I was running a library for a metals trade association, not glamour metals like gold or silver, but mundane industrial metals,—only three of them, and two were poisonous. I had been in that library for three years and decided a good career move might be to go to a special library that dealt with something more mainstream than zinc.

In the process of job hunting, I sent my resume to a major online vendor that had an opening for a trainer. To my surprise the company called me for an interview. The head of training flew to New York to interview candidates and spent an hour talking to me. It reveals my lack of self-confidence as well as interviewing skills to say that I asked very little about the nature of the job since I was convinced that the company would never hire me. The interviewer gave me a personnel form to fill out and return, which I promptly put in my desk and forgot.

Ten days later she called and asked for the form. Personnel departments seem to live for forms and have an insatiable appetite for information. If an interviewer gives out a form, personnel wants it back. Trying to put into practice some of the new things I had read about job hunting, I said, "And when were you planning to make a decision?" "Oh, I've already decided," she replied, "I'm going to hire you."

This was no time to reveal the scope of my ignorance. I accepted and two weeks later flew to California for the first time to take a job about which I knew almost nothing except the salary.

Now, ten years later, I am a salesperson for a large information company with a wide range of products and technologies from microfilm to onsite tape leasing. I cover a selected group of accounts within a geographical territory to sell the full range of our product line. At the beginning of each year my company tells me how much they expect me to sell to my accounts, and I am paid according to how well I perform against those goals. For the most part I really love it. Even on the days when the job is very taxing and frustrating and I get incensed that other people are winning my lottery money, I would be hard-pressed to think of anything else I'd rather do for a living.

NATURE OF THE WORK

Selling is very much like running your own business. The company determines what products you sell, what account base you cover and what your goals are. But how you do it is basically up to you. In most cases reps set their own schedules, make their own appointments and decide how to allocate their time and resources. Many salespeople work out of their own homes, as I do. In the beginning this was very daunting. Without the structure of an office I was afraid my days would quickly degenerate into a disturbingly intimate knowledge of the story lines for the major soaps. In reality, the opposite is true. The real problem is disciplining yourself to stop. Work is always here, under my nose, especially in a Manhattan apartment. The salespeople I know tend to spend a lot of what other people consider free time working at home. Laptops, personal copiers, answering machines, and the almighty have made it possible for one person to run a sophisticated and efficient operation out of the corner of a living room.

While selling isn't easy, it is straightforward. Your job is to find a customer who needs something you are selling, sell it to him or her, and make sure the customer's happy with it. Depending on the complexity and cost of your product or service, this process can take from a couple of hours to a couple of years. You have to find the appropriate person(s) to talk to (in libraries you often deal with committees), get them interested in your product, make an appointment to see them, present your product—often against competitive products—answer questions, follow up, submit a written proposal, follow up some more, and by the end of all this, your prospect will like what you have to offer best and buy it (you hope). Then you have to make sure it is delivered, installed, understood, serviced, upgraded—whatever—so that when you ask the prospect to buy something else, he or she will look on you and your company in a favorable light.

You spend most of your time with customers. This is the best part. You get to visit all kinds of libraries and see what they are up to. Institutions that appear remarkably similar have extremely different libraries. For example, two colleges may be geographically close, have similar curricula, student body, and budgets; yet their libraries will collect, manage, and automate in extremely divergent ways. Your products are the same, no matter which library you go to. In order to make your product interesting to the library, you have to understand that particular library's mission and operation so that the librarians can see how your product applies to their setting. This is a process of discovery. You need to understand not only the obvious operations, such as how they are automating, but also the less obvious, such as who really makes the decisions, what factors could have an effect on them, and so forth. Sometimes it's especially difficult. You may work hard to get to know an account very well, then a key person leaves and the replacement is someone who buys from your competitor. Funding sources can dry up, libraries can close. You must keep enough going with enough accounts so that someone is always buying something.

The advent of new technologies has made selling to libraries particularly challenging. Books have a tendency to stay on the shelves and behave themselves. People know how to use them. Computers, on the other hand, exhibit none of those traits. Librarians, particularly those in the public sector, have had to make rapid strides under straitened circumstances to understand and adapt to technological change. Technology is a moving target and selling it (as I do) requires a constant education process. To have credibility with your customers you must know what you are talking about. This means being able to speak knowledgeably about your products, your customer's computing environment, and your competitor's products. You don't have to be a computing wizard to do this, but you do need to have a conceptual understanding of how all these things work. And you do have to know where to find an answer when you don't have one yourself. Librarians understand that; after all, that's what they do for a living.

Librarians are extremely well educated customers. A lot of what you learn in library school is how to be a very sophisticated purchasing agent. You learn how to evaluate one reference book versus another (I got my M.L.S. before much computing was taught), how to develop a book collection, or how to select serials. Librarians need to fill their libraries, whether special, corporate, or academic, with the goods and services appropriate to their patrons' needs. Vendors are a necessary part of this process, and their salespeople call on libraries to represent their products and services.

Field representatives like me spend most of their time visiting customers. This entails calling to introduce yourself and your company, giving a busy person a compelling reason to see you, scheduling appointments within a reasonable geographic territory, and actually getting to the appointment and making the customer feel that the time spent with you was valuable. Depending on the size of the territory you cover, you may travel and frequently be away from home. You spend a lot of time, whether at home or on the road, on the telephone.

Selling also involves writing. You have to write letters and proposals, some of which can be quite lengthy. Customers need to have agreements in writing and often the salesperson is responsible for this.

You also have to account for yourself to your company. They don't just give you an expense account and say, "See you at the end of the year!" You have to submit call reports and monthly summaries of activities. The sales goals that management gives you at the beginning of the year are just not numbers picked out of a hat (although most salespeople swear they are), but part of the company's whole financial plan. Companies develop products, hire people, and enhance facilities on the basis of those projections. You have to account constantly for the piece of revenue you are responsible for bringing in. This involves forecasts, marketing plans, and, when you're desperate, a bit of wishful thinking.

QUALIFICATIONS

Sales personnel for library vendors come from a variety of backgrounds. Some companies recruit chiefly library school graduates with the assumption that sales skills can be taught. Others have the opposite approach. They recruit seasoned salespeople and teach them about libraries. Neither approach seems to dominate. Since you are visiting literate and educated customers, it's helpful, but not essential, to have a college education. Having worked as a professional librarian does, however, give you a distinct advantage. You have a working understanding of, and a professional interest in, library issues, policies, and processes. Librarians appreciate talking to someone who understands and shares their concerns and mission.

What makes a good salesperson? Most companies would like an answer to that question. There's a myth that you have to have a certain type of personality to be successful in sales. When I think of the colleagues I most respect and admire, none fits the archetype of the high-powered glad-salespeople. Good salespeople run the gamut in terms of personal style and presentation. While no one personality type seems to guarantee successful selling, there are some character traits common to most good salespeople.

The ability to work independently is essential. Most of your time is spent without direct supervision. You have to have the confidence and motivation to work alone and to provide the daily impetus to get out and do your best. This is not easy. All of us have days when we feel lousy, when personal problems seem overwhelming, and when we just don't give a damn. You still have to make calls, visit customers, and present yourself in a professional manner.

PROS AND CONS

Selling takes a lot of patience. You have to be willing to put in a lot of time with people and projects without any guarantee that you'll make a sale. You have to be persistent, even when the odds are not in your favor.

The term salesperson can conjure up very negative images for people. They think of someone who sold them something they didn't need, that didn't fit, that cost too much, that broke. Accept that the cheesy image is just part of the territory. In some ways it can work in your favor. If you are dedicated and responsive to the needs of your customers, they really appreciate it.

One of the toughest things to learn is not to take rejection personally. There's a lot of rejection in selling; you hear a lot more no than yes. People don't want to see you, don't want to buy from you, don't even want to take your phone calls. No one is immune from the bad feeling this can give you. It takes a long time to develop a philosophical attitude toward rejection and to incorporate it into your daily work life so that it has minimal effect.

What I like best about selling to libraries is that I remain involved with all aspects of my profession, from automation to collection development. Most of selling is problem solving. Good products add value to library services and enhance the effectiveness of a library's mission. I like being part of that process. I also like being able to act as an advocate for my customers, bringing ideas for product enhancement and development back to the company.

Working on your own is wonderful. Every day is different. I work long hours but have no time clock to punch. I have lots of appointments but very few meetings (the bane of working life). I love my customers and am always happiest when I'm on a sales call. New technologies and their library applications fascinate me.

I do get sick of the traveling. Selling gives you a great deal of autonomy. You purchase it, however, by dedicating a lot of personal time to the job. While your colleagues are relaxing with friends on a Friday night, you may be at some airport, cranky and exhausted, waiting for the weather to clear so your plane can take off and spirit you home.

The normal pressures and anxieties that occur when work does not go well are compounded in selling, where your income is inextricably tied to your day-to-day successes and failures. In these competitive times, maintaining your perspective on the job can be difficult, but you have to strike a balance between your professional goals and your personal life.

Would I ever go back to being a librarian? Yes. In fact, I have my retirement post already selected. There's a little library on an island on the Gulf Coast of Florida right off the beach...

CRAIG WRIGHT
RECORDS MANAGER FOR A CORPORATION

Craig Wright is employed as information specialist for Access Information Associates, Inc., 4710 Bellaire Blvd., Ste. 140, Bellaire, TX 77401. She has a B.A. from the University of Texas at Austin and an M.L.S. from Texas Woman's University. She has been active in the field of records management since 1979, including teaching records management at the University of Houston-Downtown.

INTRODUCTION

Not too many people know about records management. Tell someone you're in records management and the response may be, "You mean, phonograph records, like the Top Ten?"

The recent history of records management dates back to 1950 when the U.S. Congress passed the Federal Records Act because of the large volume of government records needing organization and preservation. The act provided the first definition of records management in a federal statute. In time, as more and more regulations were passed by the government affecting private industry, companies began to recognize a need to organize their records to comply with regulations. In short, what used to be thought of as just "filing" evolved into information MANAGEMENT. How did I learn about this field? Over a decade ago when I was a medical librarian, I began studying the employment ads in the newspaper looking for a different setting in which to use my ten years of traditional academic library experience. Eventually I saw ads that listed library science experience or education as a requirement for a position called "records analyst," a professional position in records management. A farsighted records manager took a chance on hiring me and provided on-the-job training. Thanks to her I had the opportunity to learn to do something new in the corporate sector with my old skills from the academic sector.

NATURE OF THE WORK

The primary objective of records management is making corporate records, or internal information, easily available to users by organizing and arranging them. Corporate records may include all types of media, from paper to disks and developing an index for retrieval. It sounds like library work, but there is a major difference.

Unlike libraries with cataloging rules, bibliographic controls, and published indexes, records management has no standardization, no ready-made uniform controls. Controls in records programs are established by organizing information into systems and preparing retention schedules, or timetables, for the life cycle of the data. These controls must be developed for each company and tailored for its use. Records systems and retention schedules cannot be transferred to other companies; they must be developed for each one. Records systems are developed by the records manager for each department individually, or a standard system may be developed for the entire company. Systems evolve by interviewing users of documents and data to determine what information they need to do their jobs, how they find it, and how long they need it.

The records manager is a highly visible member of the organization. In heavily regulated industries like oil and gas, this position is mandated by law. The responsibilities of the position include organizing records centers, developing schemes to index these records—possibly a standardized index for use throughout the organization, recommending the appropriate file equipment and supplies to house the records, contacting vendors for the best prices, hiring and training staff, and moving records centers from one city to another, one building to another, or just next door.

Records managers answer questions coming from anywhere in the company such as:

- "I'm cleaning out my desk; does the company have to keep these records?"

- "We're reorganizing our department and have a lot of records; how do we get rid of them?"

- "We have run out of space in our department; can you help us?"

- "We have several manually prepared lists of file folders for our area and we can't find anything anymore. Is there a better way to organize these records?"

- "There is a huge lawsuit/audit coming up. Could you help us find the documents we will need to provide quickly?"

- "We are spinning off a division of the company. Will you see that the appropriate records are transferred to the buyer?" Answers to these questions will vary depending upon the organization.

Records systems vary from industry to industry and company to company. For example, records from the banking industry are unique and serve different purposes from records of the oil and gas industry. Although organizations may have some records in common, namely personnel, tax, and financial, beyond outside those categories the similarities disappear. Records generally mirror the nature of the business.

Even within the same industry companies may be structured differently; similar departments may have different reporting relationships. In order to design a system for effective information retrieval, a records manager must understand the corporate structure, where documents originate and flow within the organization. Since corporate structure dictates the pattern for records systems, organization charts become reference tools.

Librarians have developed skills in areas that will help to offset the lack of standardization in the field of records management: the reference interview and research techniques. The reference interview, used to gain the user's participation, is essential in designing records systems and preparing retention schedules. Legal research is important to ensure the program's compliance with record keeping rules and regulations.

Retention schedules are based on two requirements: business and legal. Business requirements are identified during user interviews and usually are related to the length of time users need information. To determine legal requirements it is necessary to identify the federal, state, and local agencies that regulate the industry. Research documents such as the *Federal Register,* the *Code of Federal Regulations* and the *U.S. Statutes* that are used to identify those regulations which apply to recordkeeping for a specific industry.

The lack of standardization makes it impractical and somewhat risky to acquire a retention schedule or records system from another company or to purchase one from a vendor. Each company is unique. Each records management program must be designed to meet a specific company's needs.

Creating a records program is a demanding project. In addition to good communication and computer skills, the endeavor demands a commitment to service, a love of details, and lots of patience. It is not an overnight process.

QUALIFICATIONS

Who is in records management? What kind of training do they have? People from various educational backgrounds, with and without degrees, have found their way into this field. The literature says that organizations want people with degrees in business, computer science, business law, accounting, or human resources.(1) Occasionally an enlightened author will mention library science majors as good prospects for records management. (2) After all, librarians are versed in organizing information, using computers, and providing service. Skillful librarians combine a penchant for highly detailed work with good people skills. These are a rare combination in any occupation.

How do you learn *about* records management? Contact the Association of Records Managers and Administrators (ARMA). A professional association, it sponsors annual seminars and provides many services to support its membership. At the local level ARMA chapters offer workshops and seminars which generally are taught by experienced people from the records management community. My first introduction to records management as workshops was organized by the Houston chapter.

How do you *learn* records management? On-the-job training was the only route available for a long time. However, many junior colleges now offer courses leading to degree plans in records management. Courses are also available through the business departments at some universities and through library schools. ARMA maintains a list of colleges and universities that offer records management programs.

In addition to ARMA-sponsored seminars, classes on records management are provided throughout the United States by management consultants and training companies (contact ARMA for this list). ARMA recognizes that, as in any field, continuing education is a must. To ensure a consistent level of experience and training, ARMA has an official certifying board, the Institute of Certified Records Managers (ICRM), which administers a program for the professional certification of records managers. The ICRM is a separate organization from ARMA. By passing the six-part examination, you become a "Certified Records Manager" or CRM. The requirements to take the exam are a bachelor's degree and three years of experience in records management.

What is interesting about the experience requirement is that the ICRM board makes a special statement regarding library work. According to the ICRM brochure, "the traditional work of librarians dealing with published materials is not considered qualifying records management experience."(3) No other course of study besides library science offers indexing, cataloging and bibliographic training, which are the basics of organizing information. In my opinion, the ICRM board does not understand what librarians are trained to do. Perhaps that is our fault as librarians for not making the merits of our education better known.

PROS AND CONS

On the positive side records managers have a broader range of responsibilities than you may have thought. They include negotiating contracts for records storage, imaging equipment maintenance, and moving companies; hiring, firing, and training personnel; budgeting; recommending and purchasing filing equipment and supplies, imaging equipment, computers, and software. Records managers are space planners, policy makers, writers, and salesmen. They are also educators because their supervisors often do not understand records management. The rewards are higher visibility in the organization, greater responsibility, and higher salaries than many corporate librarians.

Opportunities for employment in records management are numerous when you consider that all companies and institutions, whether they realize it or not, must keep records. Private industry, particularly heavily regulated industries, must have records management programs. Government is another arena for opportunities in records management. The federal government's department is the National Archives and Records Administration (NARA). (NARA also offers many records management seminars.) State and local governments have similar departments, although they may be affiliated with the state archives or library. Consulting, too, is experiencing a growing demand from companies which either have no records management department or are understaffed.

A librarian employed as a corporate records manager may have the opportunity to provide a one-stop information service by combining internal information (records) with external information (publications and databases). In this economic climate, combining similar services when possible provides a savings to the organization.(4) Libraries are often perceived by management as costly, but by purchasing printed materials on demand only, using databases whenever possible, and employing fewer people, libraries can change this perception. When user demands become too heavy, farm out the work to consultants. Make information services available to users throughout the organization on a worldwide basis.

As the world shrinks and more companies become multinational, demand will rise for information organizers in other countries. It's not unusual for a records manager based in Houston to travel to Nigeria or Singapore to oversee the records reorganization and staff training in those offices. Remember, all organizations have records; not all organizations have libraries.

As for the negatives because the image of records management may still be that of filing, some librarians may not hold records management in high esteem. Nevertheless, corporate librarians often report to records managers, degrees notwithstanding. The reason for this, I believe, is that higher-level managers perceive the records manager as a greater risk taker than the librarian. For those used to traditional settings and bibliographic controls, the unstructured environment of records management may seem risky. However, nobody is as well-prepared for records management as you. Take the plunge!

APPENDIX

Association of Records Manager and Administrators (ARMA)
4200 Somerset Drive, Suite 215
Prairie Village, KS 66208
800-422-ARMA; FAX 913-341-3742

Institute of Certified Records Managers (ICRM)
P.O. Box 8188
Prairie Village, KS 66208
800-825-ICRM

REFERENCES

1. Ricks, Betty R.; Swafford, Ann J.; Gow, Kay E. *Information and image management.* 3rd edition. Cincinnati: South-Western Publishing; 1992. p. 38.

2. Wright, Craig. Corporate records management and the librarian. *Special Libraries.* 82(4):300–304; 1991 Fall.

3. Institute of Certified Records Managers. *Certified records manager.* Prairie Village, KS; 1989 January. See section under "Librarianship."

4. Wright, Craig W. The corporate information challenge: streamlining external information. *Records Management Quarterly.* 25(3):14–16; 1991 July.

INDEX